THE
NEW
Pekingese

Ch. St. Aubrey Carnival Music of Eastfield, Ch. St. Aubrey Fairy Ku of Craigfoss, and Eng. Am. Can. Ch. Goofus Bugatti. *Portrait by Cherie Williamson Rush, 1969*

THE
NEW
Pekingese

Nigel Aubrey-Jones

With special contributions by
R. William Taylor and Andrew H. Brace

HOWELL
BOOK HOUSE
New York

Collier Macmillan Canada
Toronto

Maxwell Macmillan International
New York   Oxford   Singapore   Sydney

Howell Book House
Macmillan Publishing Company
866 Third Avenue, New York, NY 10022

Collier Macmillan Canada, Inc.
1200 Eglinton Avenue East, Suite 200
Don Mills, Ontario M3C 3N1

Library of Congress Cataloging-in-Publication Data
Aubrey-Jones, Nigel.
      The new Pekingese/Nigel Aubrey-Jones; with special contributions by R. William
   Taylor and Andrew H. Brace.
          p.   cm.
      Includes bibliographical references (p.   ).
      ISBN 0-87605-222-7
      1. Pekingese dog.   I. Taylor, R. William.   II. Brace, Andrew H.   III. Title.
   SF429.P3A93   1990
   636.7′6—dc20   90-4819   CIP

Macmillan books are available at special discounts for bulk purchases for sales
promotions, premiums, fund-raising, or educational use. For details, contact:

                              Special Sales Director
                              Macmillan Publishing Company
                              866 Third Avenue
                              New York, NY 10022

10 9 8 7 6 5 4 3 2 1

Printed in the United States of America

To my partner,
R. William Taylor,
for whom I have had so much
to be thankful

An informal snapshot of two beautiful bitches resident at the Cambalu Kennel of Marjorie Kaye and Richard Kruger: Ch. Cambalu Sunburst Crystal (top) and her daughter, Ch. Cambalu Hurly Burly.

Contents

The author with Am. & Can. Ch. St. Aubrey Yorklee Fanfare Royale. *Thomas Fall*

About the Author

by Andrew H. Brace

NIGEL AUBREY-JONES is the most qualified individual in the world today to write a book on Pekingese. Originally registered with the Kennel Club, England, in the 1930s by his father, Aubrey-Jones's St. Aubrey affix has become synonymous with the highest quality in Pekingese and has been carried by many legendary specimens of the breed on both sides of the Atlantic.

In partnership with R. William Taylor, Mr. Aubrey-Jones's St. Aubrey-Elsdon Kennel has housed many of the great names in contemporary Pekingese history, and dogs bred, sold or owned by him have accounted for almost one thousand Best in Show awards.

As a canine journalist, the author is acknowledged as one of the leaders in the field. Over the past thirty-five years he has contributed to *Dog World, Dog News* and *Kennel Review,* as well as *Dog World* and *Dogs Monthly* in the United Kingdom. He edited *Popular Dogs* magazine at one time and published both *The Dog Fancier* and *Pekingese Parade.*

Proprietor of Bibliography of the Dog, he handles fine art, paintings, bronzes, rare books and prints, and his private collection of Pekingese literature and artifacts is possibly the finest in the world.

Much in demand the world over, Mr. Aubrey-Jones is recognized as one of the Pekingese breed's most authoritative judges. Judging Pekingese and other breeds has taken him all over the world.

Few authors of a breed book are in a position to draw on half a century of personal experience and success, which fact brings to this title a rare individuality.

THE PEKINESE
NATIONAL ANTHEM

BY

E. V. LUCAS

ILLUSTRATED BY PERSIS KIRMSE

METHUEN & CO. LTD.
36 ESSEX STREET W.C.
LONDON

This is the front cover of *The Pekinese National Anthem* by E.V. Lucas, which was originally published in England in 1930. This charming work was issued in the form of an illustrated booklet with drawings by Persis Kirmse, sister to the celebrated illustrator Marguerite Kirmse, who lived and worked in the United States and whose work is popular among collectors of dog art. *The Pekinese National Anthem* is reproduced in its entirety on pages xi, xii and xiv of this book. Note the old spelling of the breed name in the title.

THE PEKINESE
NATIONAL ANTHEM

The Pekinese
Disdain to please
  On any set design,
But make a thrall
Of one and all
  By simple Right Divine.

The Pekinese
Our houses seize
  And mould them till they suit,
For every one
's Napoleon
  And Wellington to
    boot.

The Pekinese
Demosthenes
    Requires no voice to plead :
Those shining eyes,
So soft, so wise,
    Get everything they need.

The Pekinese
Abstain from fleas
    And doggy things like that,
But hate it when
Unthinking men
    Compare them to the cat.

The Pekinese
From autumn trees
    Their colour scheme obtain ;
    And all their lives
    Their frugal wives
        From any change refrain.

The Pekinese
Have feathered knees,
    And plumes where tails should be,
And as they race
About the place
    They ripple like the sea.

Acknowledgments

To say that the writing of this book has been a great effort would be a gross understatement.

I doubt that anyone has had as much pleasure from this breed or has had the good fortune to have owned so many great Pekingese.

Further, I recall with great affection and gratitude the many outstanding Pekingese breeders I have met over the years, several of whom became personal friends. Their experience and knowledge helped shape my own opinions in my formative years.

For almost fifty years this breed has made my life full, exciting and successful.

I was indeed fortunate in meeting my partner of forty years, R. William Taylor, whose enthusiasm, help and patience have made this great romance with the Pekingese a glorious experience. A very special thank-you to Andrew Brace, a great admirer of the breed, for the tremendous effort he has contributed in helping to put this book together.

NIGEL AUBREY-JONES
Montreal

The Pekinese,
Although such wees,
  Are destitute of fear ;
Both fleet and strong,
They bound along,
  As buoyant as the deer.

The Pekinese
Say ' Bread and cheese
  Will do for such as you ;
For us a fare
More choice and rare,
  And jolly punctual too.'

The Pekinese
Adore their ease
  And slumber like the dead ;
    In comfort curled
    They view the world
      As one unending bed.

The Pekinese
On China's seas
  Embarked to win the West ;
A piece of Ming
's a lovely thing,
  But oh ! the dogs are best.

THE
NEW
Pekingese

Looty, who died in 1872, was one of the Pekingese discovered in the Summer Palace, Pekin, on its occupation by the Allied Forces in 1860. Looty was presented by General Dunne to Her Majesty Queen Victoria.

Pekin Prince was imported to Britain by Mrs. Loftus Allen in 1896.

1

The Origin and History of the Pekingese

TO MY KNOWLEDGE there have been in excess of one hundred books published on this, the most fascinating of breeds. In most of these will be found countless legends and fables as to the origins of the "Lion Dog of Peking."

When you acquire a Pekingese, you are acquiring more than a dog. You are in possession of the culmination of many years' selective breeding at the Chinese Court and beyond; its history has become intertwined with legend and romance. Your Pekingese is a unique legacy.

Royal Isolation

Pekingese were little known in China, other than in Peking (Beijing) itself, and even there were never sighted outside the precincts of the Royal Palace. The punishment meted out to anyone found removing a Pekingese from its regal home was usually death by stoning or other, equally barbaric methods. Consequently, very few early Pekingese got beyond the palace walls, and so the favored little dogs remained in their stately home for centuries, unhindered by influences of the outside world.

Sacking of the Summer Palace

As the Manchu dynasty came to an end, political turmoil was rife in China, largely due to the Empress's hatred of the "foreign devil" (European colonial influences). During one crisis in 1860 the Emperor, encouraged by the Empress,

Mr. and Mrs. T. Douglas Murray's Ah Cum and Mimosa were obtained from the Imperial Palace and died in 1905 and 1909 respectively.

The original Goodwood Pekingese, Guh and Meh, brought from Pekin after the looting of the Summer Palace and presented to the Duchess of Richmond and Gordon.

aroused the anger of the Western nations, which resulted in their marching on the summer palace outside Peking. The royal household fled, taking with them all possessions including the precious and revered "Lion Dogs," but in their haste five such dogs were left behind and these subsequently fell into the hands of British officers. A now-famous little parti-color was secured by General Dunne and upon his return to England was presented to Queen Victoria who, appropriately, named her "Looty."

Looty was small, perhaps weighing no more than five pounds. Indeed, none of these five original dogs weighed more than six pounds, which would suggest that the original palace dogs were all quite small. Subsequently, the other remaining dogs from the looting found their way to England, Lord John Hay returning with a pair and the last pair being presented to the Duke and Duchess of Richmond.

The Pekingese's British Conquest

Not surprisingly, interest in the newly arrived Oriental grew rapidly in Britain, and much effort went into importing more specimens of the charming breed from its homeland. Times were changing in China, and so Pekingese, for so many years prisoners within the palace walls, were now given as prized gifts to a favored few, though such gifts were bestowed in small numbers.

The early imports to Britain are all well documented, though in view of the rapid increase in numbers it could be assumed that imports arrived of which nothing is known.

In the 1890s Pekingese existed in Britain in such numbers that showing them in competition became a viable proposition. Pekin Peter was imported by Loftus Allen in 1893, and he was exhibited at the Chester show the following year—the first time a member of the breed appeared in a British show ring. Pekin Prince and Pekin Princess followed in 1896, and thus the foundations of the Pekin strain were laid. Both of these, incidentally, were black.

The Duke of Richmond had earlier started the Goodwood Kennel, which was subsequently taken over by Lord and Lady Algernon Lennox, and they produced some of the best of the earlier specimens. For many years Goodwood was regarded as the fountainhead of the breed in Britain.

Also in 1896 the famous Ah Cum and Mimosa were imported to Britain directly from the Imperial Palace by Mrs. T. Douglas Murray, and thus her palace strain was established.

The Pekingese rapidly developed a higher profile among the dog-showing fancy, and originally the breed's interests were catered to by the Japanese Spaniel Club, which in 1898 drew up the first Standard of points for the Pekingese. The year 1904 saw the founding of the Pekingese Club; its aim was to promote a small, compact dog under ten pounds in weight and of the type found in the specimens removed from the Imperial Palace. No weight limit was enforced, but four years later some members, believing that the breed was in danger of losing the "palace" type, broke away from the parent club to found the Pekin Palace

Ch. Goodwood Chun gave his name to the deep red color so seldom seen nowadays.

Mrs. Douglas Murray's Ch. Goodwood Lo, the very first Pekingese champion and considered outstanding in his day.

Sutherland Oeun-Teu Tang was the litter brother to Ch. Chu-Erh of Alderbourne, and from these two brothers developed two distinct lines. However, after World War II, Tang's line virtually disappeared.

An early Manchu champion, Manchu Cheng-Tu, a prolific prizewinner for Lady Decies.

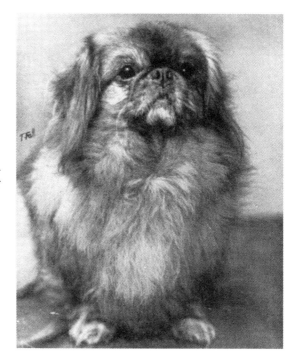

Mrs. Sealy Clarke's Ch. Broadoak Beetle weighed eight and a half pounds and became a key stud dog. Among its immediate progeny was Ch. Ko-Tzu of Burderop.

Mrs. Kennedy's homebred Ch. Nanking Wen Ti, born in 1908, was a son of Sutherland Ouen Teu Tang. He was one of the dogs responsible for developing the desirable flatness of face in the Pekingese.

Dog Association. For many years one could only exhibit dogs up to ten pounds in weight at the Association's shows, and to this day many trophies and cups offered by the Association are open only to exhibits that comply with this maximum weight.

Beginnings of American Activity

It is often mistakenly assumed that the Pekingese in America is exclusively the result of early importations from Britain, yet we know that as early as 1903 direct Chinese imports were being exhibited in the United States.

The Pekingese Club of America was founded in 1909, and the Standard was the same as that adopted in Great Britain, though the original American Standard listed eighteen pounds as a disqualification, with the suggestion that when classes were divided by weight they should be classified as up to ten pounds and under ten pounds. Today's breed Standard in America specifies a maximum weight of fourteen pounds.

With the fall of the Manchu dynasty in 1911 and the resulting revolution, the great majority of Pekingese were destroyed by the court officials, with the result that, a few years later, the breed was virtually extinct in the land that had nurtured it for so many generations. However, in its adopted homeland the Pekingese grew from strength to strength, swiftly climbing the popularity polls, in no small measure due to the fact that the breed's image was blessed by the favor of royalty and the nobility. Half a world away, its own imperial heritage was still very much a part of the Pekingese's attraction.

A great debt of gratitude is owed to the early British Pekingese breeders who developed the breed to such a high standard, enabling fanciers in the United States and elsewhere to acquire quality foundation stock on which they, in turn, could build.

Mention has been made of the Goodwood, Pekin and Palace kennels, which really were the foundation of the breed in Britain. The first Pekingese champion there was Goodwood Lo, followed by Goodwood Chun (which gave its name to the "chun red" color seldom seen, alas, in the show ring today). Both dogs were prolific sires and had a great influence on the breed in those early days. Several kennels were founded on these original bloodlines, which were subsequently to become world-famous in their own right; the Manchu, Broadoak, Sutherland Avenue, Nanking and Burderop spring readily to mind, along with, arguably the most famous of all, Alderbourne, the kennel that continued to be active right up until the 1960s.

From these early cornerstone kennels grew many lines and kennels that were to found their own dynasties in turn, and of whom more will be heard later.

Having caught the imagination of the American dog fancier, many British imports were brought across the Atlantic by pioneers of the breed, such as J. Pierpont Morgan, Mrs. Morris Mandy, Mrs. Michael van Beuren, Mrs. M. E. Harby and Lydia K. Hopkins.

The appeal of the Pekingese in the United States was spurred on when Mrs.

Nicholas Longworth (then Alice Roosevelt, daughter of President Theodore Roosevelt) received one of the palace dogs when she visited China, and we are told that Mrs. E. H. Conger, wife of the American minister to China, had also been made a gift of a Pekingese by the Dowager Empress herself.

The foundations having been set in Britain and America, at the turn of the century the breed was in a strong position for the future. There would be no further importation of consequence from the land of the breed's birth. The Pekingese's future rested with those who had chosen to adopt it, armed only with their knowledge of the breed's history, their inherent aptitude for breeding livestock, their eye for quality and a vision of the Pekingese of the future.

Mrs. Calley's celebrated winner, Ch. Ko-Tzu of Burderop.

2

The Pekingese
Comes to America

IT IS RECORDED that the first person to exhibit a Pekingese in America was Mrs. George Thomas, who showed one of the breed in the Miscellaneous class at Philadelphia in 1901. It was not until 1906 that the American Kennel Club authorized breed classes for Pekingese, and the first show to schedule the breed was run by the Toy Spaniel Club. It should be remembered that at this time the breed was officially known as the "Pekingese Spaniel," a name it maintained for several years. At this first historical scheduling of the breed in its own right, the noted judge James Mortimer officiated, and his choice for Best of Breed was Mrs. Morris Mandy's T'sang of Downshire. Mrs. Mandy began breeding Pekingese in England, and after settling in America did much to further the breed on this side of the Atlantic. Subsequently T'sang of Downshire became the first champion for the breed in the United States, while the first bitch to become titled was Dr. Mary Cotton's Chaou Ching-Ur. Interestingly, Dr. Cotton's bitch was actually bred by the Dowager Empress and imported directly from China.

The Pekingese Club of America

Having been formed in 1909, the Pekingese Club of America held its first Specialty show in 1911 at the Plaza Hotel in New York, the venue that was to be its home for several years. In such glittering surroundings, the show was a great social success and the judge-elect was Mrs. Benjamin Guinness, president of the Club at the time. Her Winners Dog was T'sang of Downshire, while the

Mrs. Morris Mandy's Tsang of Downshire won Best of Breed in 1906 when Pekingese were first given breed classes in the United States, and subsequently became the breed's first champion in America.

Dr. Mary Cotton's Chaou Ching-Ur was actually bred by the Dowager Empress and, having been imported to America, became the first champion bitch.

Mrs. Paul Sorg's Ch. Broadoak Fatima, an imported daughter of Ch. Broadoak Beetle, was Winners Bitch at the first Specialty show held by the Pekingese Club of America in 1911.

Cairnwhin Tinto was imported into America by Mrs. A. L. Holland from the eminent English breeder, Lefroy Dean, who subsequently made her Winners Bitch at the 1917 Pekingese Club of America specialty.

11

Winners Bitch was Mrs. Paul Sorg's Broadoak Fatima, an imported daughter of the key English male, Ch. Broadoak Beetle.

The Pekingese Club of America shows held at the ballroom of the Plaza were undoubtedly splendid affairs, with the list of exhibitors being reminiscent of a page from the Social Register. They were obviously society events as much as canine competitions, and the publicity they attracted was vast—as were the entries. The New York newspapers covered the events in depth—though whether they were as interested in the Pekingese as the people who owned them is a debatable point—and it was obvious that the Pekingese had earned itself a place in America's fashionable circles. The Pekingese was not an inexpensive commodity. Puppies can be found for sale in Pekingese Club of America catalogs from the 1910s at $500. The entries at the Club Specialties of this period were also staggering: 289 Pekingese were entered at the 1914 show. Compare that number with the total of over one hundred received for the 1990 Speciality.

The 1917 Specialty produced a story well worth telling. The judge was an eminent English breeder, LeFroy Dean, from whom Mrs. A. L. Holland had purchased her bitch, Cairnwhin Tinto. Quite within the rules, Tinto was entered under Mr. Dean and performed beautifully until she heard Mr. Dean's voice, whereupon she made a rush for her former owner. She finally settled to give a polished performance that resulted in her receiving the Winners award. It is reported that, during judging, Mr. Dean was seen to be wiping away tears, yet he remained stoic until he had completed his assignment. However, when the last ribbon had been presented to Mrs. Holland, Mr. Dean scooped up Tinto, hugged her unashamedly and let the tears stream. It must have been a most emotional moment for all concerned.

A Vignette of History

Another interesting story of the period does not concern the Pekingese Club of America but does deserve a place in the breed's history. At the Westminster show of 1918 the Best in Show competition was between the Pekingese Ch. Phantom of Ashcroft and a Bull Terrier, Ch. Haymarket Faultless. Two judges, Charles Hopton and Vinton Breese, had the job of deciding Best. Hopton preferred the Pekingese while Breese favored the Bull Terrier. Neither gentleman would back down, and the chain of events were such that at times it was believed the judges would resort to physical violence. Each severely criticized the other's choice, and much argument accompanied the proceedings. Evidently the judging took several hours, and eventually the referee, George Thomas, was called in to break the deadlock—the final decision went to the Bull Terrier. We are told that all three judges were subsequently suspended!

Notable Early Fanciers

One of the breed's early patrons in America was J. Pierpont Morgan, a gentleman of considerable wealth. On a trip to England he was captivated by the charms of Mrs. Clarice Ashton Cross's Ch. Chu-Erh of Alderbourne, which was

Ch. Chu-Erh of Alderbourne, the first champion for this historic kennel and the dog for whom J. Pierpont Morgan offered $50,000—and was refused!

Mrs. Michael van Beuren's Prince Kung of Alderbourne with daughters Kuna and Taku.

whelped in 1905. He originally offered $15,000, then $37,500, and then $50,000—all of which were refused. In desperation the persistent Mr. Morgan sent a blank check, which Mrs. Ashton Cross also returned. So impressed was one newspaper of the day with this amazing story that it carried an article that claimed there were three things in England that even Pierpont Morgan could not buy: good weather, a British policeman and Mrs. Ashton Cross's dog!

Guardians of the breed in America in these early days also included Lydia Hopkins, who owned the Sherwood Kennel; Mrs. Harry Sears of the Wu Kees; the Greenwich Kennel of Mrs. F. Y. Mathis; the Whitworth Kennel of Mr. and Mrs. Herbert Mapes; the F. C. McAllisters and Mrs. Christian Hager of the Chu Chows. The vast majority of the early breeders was based on the East Coast, but the fruits of their labors soon found their way to other parts of the country.

Following in their footsteps came a new generation of fanciers of the caliber of Mrs. Michael van Beuren, for many years president of the Pekingese Club of America. She imported winners from leading English strains and also owned the jet black Pier Wan Li of Orchard Hill, which was bred and handled by Dorothy Quigley, herself one of the leading authorities of the subsequent period. Mr. and Mrs. Frank Downing brought in several outstanding imports that, when combined with existing American lines, produced many champions at their Hollylodge Kennel. Bertha Hanson owned the successful O'Palarts, while Mrs. James Austin imported some of the best stock in England, breeding many winners at her Catawba establishment. When Mrs. Austin died, tragedy doubly befell American Pekingese because her veterinarian was ordered to put all her dogs to sleep.

Ruth Burnette Sayres was one-time kennel manager for Mrs. Austin and after her death showed Poodles for Mrs. Saunders Meade. Not surprisingly, Mrs. Sayres' enthusiasm for Pekingese was soon shared by Mrs. Meade, who was encouraged to buy the magnificent British import Ch. Caversham Ko Ko of Shanruss.

Of all the early breeders in this country, none built up a distinct strain more definitely than Sara Hodges of the Dah Wongs. Keeping to a tight breeding program within her own kennel, she produced Pekingese that were known for their beautiful heads and sturdy conformation.

While several British breeders have been successful in establishing a definite ''type'' to such an extent that their dogs can be seen from ringside and immediately their breeding can be identified, fewer American breeders have succeeded in doing so. Great Britain is such a physically small country that any stud dog can be visited after a relatively short trip. Thus British breeders have been able to avail themselves of the best and, more important, the most suitable stud dogs with little personal inconvenience. Breeding to the best in America is not so easy.

Lest readers should take issue with the above, it must be understood that the breed Standard requirements are such that there can exist ''types'' within a breed, all equally correct yet quite distinctive. Provided they satisfy the essentials of the breed Standard, it is not for us to say which, if any, is better.

Eng. & Am. Ch. Che Le of Matson's Catawba, owned by Mrs. James Austin, was the first multiple Best in Show winner in the United States and is pictured in 1942 being handled by Ruth Burnette Sayres.

Eng. & Am. Ch. Caversham Ko Ko of Shanruss winning Best in Show at Westchester Kennel Club in 1955. Shown with R. William Taylor and Nigel Aubrey-Jones.

The Misses Clara and Margaretta Lowther owned the Clamarlow Kennel, which was responsible for many Specialty winners. John Royce and his sister Caroline established the Dah Lyn Kennel in 1929, and "Jack" Royce's knowledge of pedigrees was used to advantage by many aspiring breeders. Of his many imports, Ch. Kai Jin of Caversham was a multiple Best in Show winner and a sire of no mean significance. His homebred bitch, Ch. Kai Lo of Dah Lyn, is remembered with admiration by many senior enthusiasts, and her show record at the time was quite formidable.

In New England, kennels such as the Heskeths of Mrs. Hadaway and Mrs. French Williams sprang up, while in Texas Mrs. Murray Brooks's Tien Hias fielded a strong team for many years. Mrs. Brooks's breeding program incorporated much of the Caversham breeding introduced to the United States by Dorothy Quigley, who, incidentally, was one of the first American judges to officiate in Great Britain, along with John Royce and Ruth Burnette Sayres.

Charmian Lansdowne went to California from England in the 1930s, bringing with her the foundation of her Cha Ming Kennel. At about the same time, Peggy Bielot's Punchinello Kennel was born in Detroit, the location of Marilyn Buktus's Golden Gay Kennel, later taken over by her daughter Adele.

Muriel Freyman was an important breeder in the Midwest, bringing in good English stock and always maintaining a strong kennel of bitches at Pekeholme. In the same area, Mrs. Daniel Goodwin and Amber Darville both kept kennels whose bloodlines were based on Dorothy Quigley's Orchard Hills, as did Mrs. N. E. Leedy.

The Herbert Mapeses remained in prominence with their Whitworth Kennels for many years until the death in 1955 of Mrs. Mapes, a talented painter of Pekingese. Herbert Mapes spent his latter years with their niece, Mrs. Fortune Roberts, who herself became a judge of Pekingese before she died in the 1980s.

Mrs. Everett Clark of New York established a strain of American-bred stock under the Miralac name, while the Rosedowns of Evelyn Ortega enjoyed success with homebred and imported stock alike. The Del Vilas of sisters Mrs. Justin Herold and Delphine McEntyre came to prominence in the 1950s, though they founded their kennel some years before. Mrs. Edwin Blamey's Millrose Kennel was Long Island–based; her husband was the official veterinarian for the Pekingese Club of America as far back as 1920.

Mrs. Herbert Katz of Syracuse quickly achieved success with her large Roh Kai Kennel, handling her own dogs and later acquiring imported stock such as Ch. St. Aubrey Kimono of Tzumiao, a Best in Show winner of the early 1950s. Another kennel to import successfully from Great Britain was that of Mrs. Clifford Bailie, her Ch. Montgomery of Alderbourne combining well with specially imported bitches.

In Delaware, Hermine Cleaver handled several prolific winners, and the Dragon Hai Kennel of Harold Frazer and Allen Williams enjoyed success prior to their leaving for Australia.

Bettina Belmont Ward imported from England Black Queen of Orchard House, the bitch having been bred to Ch. Caversham Ku Ku of Yam, the British

The Misses Lathrop's Beh Tang seen winning Best of Breed in Westminster in 1943 under Dorothy Quigley. This bitch won the Group later that day.

sensation. The result of this importation was Ch. Bettina's Kow Kow, the winner of more than twenty Bests in Show.

The Tennessee-based kennel of Houston and Peggy Dillard Carr has been in existence for forty years, and another long-standing fancier is Mrs. Russell Inge, who bought from Mrs. Quigley Ch. St. Aubrey Judy of Calartha, the British champion she obtained from me. She won seven Challenge Certificates (three being needed for a U.K. championship, and those to be won under three different judges, at least one after the recipient's first birthday. Remember, too, that in Britain there is no equivalent to our Winners Dog; to take the "CC" a dog must beat all the champions present) and then obtained her title in Canada and the United States.

The St. Aubrey Story

Reluctant as I am to catalog the successes of dogs that I obtained in Britain and that subsequently came to the United States carrying our St. Aubrey affix, to omit them would create a false picture of the breed's progress here because many of them became significant winners and producers in various different ownerships.

Judy was the first Pekingese to carry the St. Aubrey affix in the United States, and she was followed by Pu Chi of Perryacre, a Challenge Certificate winner in Britain, that was sold to Mrs. Quigley. St. Aubrey Tai Chuo of Charterway was sold to Mr. and Mrs. Charles C. Venable, being preceded by the all-breed Best in Show winning Eng. Ch. Caversham Ko Ko of Shanruss, which was bought by Mrs. Saunders Meade. Ko Ko won Best in Show at the 1955 Westchester Kennel Club show, at that time owned by me and my partner of some forty years, R. William Taylor, whose Elsdon Pekingese were established in Canada before the two kennels merged.

In 1956 we imported to Canada the exciting young British dog, Chik T'sun of Caversham, bought from Mary de Pledge and Herminie Lunham. He was a Reserve Challenge Certificate winner in England but in Canada progressed to win Dog of the Year for 1956. By the end of the year he was sold to the Venables, who placed him in the hands of the eminent Toy handler Clara Alford. In 1957 he won the first of three Toy Groups at Westminster, taking Best in Show there in 1960. In total Chik T'sun won 126 Bests in Show and 169 Group firsts in the United States, and for many years this record made him the biggest-winning show dog in American history for all breeds. To this day he remains the top-winning Pekingese of all time. Only two Pekingese have won Best at Westminster since. In 1982 Ch. St. Aubrey Dragonora of Elsdon won, and in 1990 it was Ch. Wendessa Crown Prince who reigned supreme, his pedigree being partly St. Aubrey-Elsdon on both sire's and dam's side.

The next significant male for me to bring to the States was Ch. Calartha Mandarin of Jehol, sold to Vera F. Crofton. Arriving in the late 1950s, Mandarin became a prepotent sire of Best in Show and Group-winning Pekingese. He was succeeded by his son, Ch. Rikki of Calartha, who also won his title in Canada, again owned by Vera Crofton. Like his sire, Rikki more than proved himself as

Mary de Pledge with Ch. Caversham Ko Ko of Shanruss (left), the judge of the breed, Mrs. Dadachanji, and Nigel Aubrey-Jones with Ch. St. Aubrey Judy of Calartha, winning the Challenge Certificates at an English show in 1950. Mr. Aubrey-Jones subsequently brought both these great champions to the United States.

Eng. & Am. Ch. Chik T'Sun of Caversham was bred by Mary de Pledge and Herminie Lunham, and imported by Nigel Aubrey-Jones and R. William Taylor. Later sold to Mr. and Mrs. Charles C. Venable, the dog is shown here winning its first BIS in the United States. For many years Chik T'Sun held the record for the top-winning show dog of any breed in America.

a stud dog, and this father-son duo had great influence on the breed during this Golden Age of Pekingese.

Ch. St. Aubrey Jin T'sun of Holmvallee then came over and was sold to Charleen Prescott and Audrey A. Atherton, who ensured that he was used to advantage. Mrs. Crofton then acquired a son of Rikki, Ch. St. Aubrey Seminole of Wanstrow, later to become a Best in Show and Group winner for her. I then obtained the British champion Calartha Wee Bo Bo of Ecila. He became a Best in Show winner in Canada before joining Mrs. Crofton's kennel.

Ch. St. Aubrey Yung Derrie of Soozan was the next dog to be bought in England, where so many outstanding Pekingese could be found at the time, and he too was sold to Mrs. Crofton. Ch. St. Aubrey Ku Kuan of Jehol became a more than useful stud dog for Nell Bailey. Meanwhile, another British champion had been procured: Ch. Calartha Yen Lo of Sualane, a son of Rikki. He went to Mrs. Gerald Livingston of New York.

In 1967 the St. Aubrey-Elsdon Kennel transferred to Great Britain where my partner and I remained until our return to Montreal in 1974. Prior to our leaving for the United Kingdom, the kennel had been more or less disbanded. We continued breeding and exhibiting when in England, but it was a year after we returned, in 1975, that I made what is undoubtedly considered the most important find of many years of Pekingese watching in Britain. I write of discovering the outstandingly successful sire, Ch. St. Aubrey Laparata Dragon, of which much more will be heard later, because his part in the play of the contemporary American Pekingese is without doubt outstanding.

More Old Friends

Returning to those breeders and kennels who are no longer regularly campaigning but who played their part in the middle of the century in developing the modern Pekingese, Horace Wilhoite of Alabama founded a kennel on quality English lines complemented with already established American strains. He had a special affection for black Pekingese.

Mr. and Mrs. Paul Ausman owned the Pa We Ja Kennel and enjoyed an excellent run with one of their first homebreds, Ch. Ku Kan Jin, sired by the English import Ch. Jamestown Kai Jin of Caversham.

Vivian Longacre first began her love affair with the Pekingese in 1936, and her El Acre Kennel housed such dogs as the Best in Show Ch. Che Fon.

Not all fanciers and supporters of the Pekingese were necessarily large-scale breeders, but their contribution was nonetheless valuable. Kitty Duff of Ohio, for example, took much pride in owning beautiful Pekingese but never wished to keep a large breeding kennel.

Ruth and Irving Livingston imported several big-winning dogs direct from England's Coughton and Copplestone kennels. The Chun Chun Fu Kennel of Shirley Stone was a successful contemporary, one whose notoriety in recent times was perhaps not of the sort its late owner would have wished. On Shirley Stone's death her kennel and dogs were put up for auction by the next of kin.

20

Ch. Calartha Mandarin of Jehol, brought to the United States and owned by Vera F. Crofton. Mandarin became a prepotent sire of Group and Best in Show winners.

The British-bred son of Mandarin, Ch. Rikki of Calartha, imported by Nigel Aubrey-Jones and R. William Taylor and owned by Vera Crofton.

Eng. & Am. Ch. Calartha Wee Bo Bo of Ecila was another Mandarin son imported by St. Aubrey-Elsdon and sold to Vera Crofton.

Ch. St. Aubrey Mayfly of Allenvale was a British import and is seen here winning Best of Breed at Chicago in the late 1950s under Edward B. McQuown; handled by owner Edna Voyles.

In the early 1950s the Mar Pat Kennel of Martha Bingham (now Mrs. Victor Olmos-Olivier) and her sister, Patricia Miller, was formed, and at its height housed a large number of champions. Today Mrs. Olmos-Olivier concentrates her canine activities on judging.

It is impossible to catalog everyone who has made a contribution to the breed in this country because there are many aficionados of the Pekingese whose activities, however modest, have in some way sown the seeds for future generations to reap.

A champion in Britain, the United States and Canada, Ch. Goofus Bugatti was shown in the ownership of Nigel Aubrey-Jones, R. William Taylor and Vera Crofton and handled by Clara Alford in the United States where he was a Westminster Best of Breed winner. He also took Best of Breed at Crufts—possibly a unique "double."

Eng. Ch. Mathilda of Kettlemere was imported to the United States by St. Aubrey-Elsdon, became an American champion and was owned by Gilma Blauvelt-Moss.

3

The Modern Pekingese in America

IF WE CONSIDER the "modern" Pekingese to refer to the breed over the past forty years, the scene was set by the early breeders covered in the preceding chapter. The basis was there on which the new generation was to build, and as I contemplate this era, my mind goes back to one of the greatest tragedies of the time as far as the Pekingese breed is concerned.

In the forties the beautiful Eng. Ch. Yusen Yu Toi had been purchased by Dorothy Quigley from his breeder, Sally Higgs. Tragically, Yu Toi died in transit, and so we can only speculate as to how profound an influence he would have exerted on the modern Pekingese in America and whether or not that influence would have resulted in the breed taking a slightly different direction. As some compensation, however, Mrs. Quigley was fortunate enough to import a son of Yu Toi, namely Int. Ch. Bonraye Fo Yu of Orchard Hill, which built up an admirable record of show wins. He was, in fact, the first postwar British champion Pekingese to come to America. As mentioned earlier, Ch. St. Aubrey Judy of Calartha came to the United States with her British title, as did Ch. Caversham Ko Ko of Shanruss. The next British champion to cross the Atlantic was Ch. Merio of Ifield, obtained by Doris Ostling, followed by Ch. Tong Tuo of Pekeboro, which was bought by Mrs. Horace H. Wilson. He finished his British title in 1956. The early 1960s saw the arrival of Ch. Calartha Wee Bo Bo of Ecila, a son of Mandarin who was already in the United States. He was followed by the Mandarin grandson, Ch. Calartha Yen Lo of Sualane. In the mid-sixties, Ch. Fu Yong of Jamestown gave Charleen Prescott a British champion in her kennel, and he was followed by Ch. Jinette of Jamestown. My partner and I bought the Eng. Ch. Goofus Bugatti after he had obtained his title and Best of Breed at Crufts; we took him to Canada and from there he completed his U.S. and Canadian championships. When we returned to England, Bugatti came too and added another Challenge Certificate at the Pekingese Club Championship show. Another British champion to cross the Atlantic in the sixties was Ch. Alderbourne Li Fu of Remward, bought by Lloyd Stacey. I then brought across Ch. Mathilda of Kettlemere who later went to Mrs. Gilma Blauvelt-Moss.

In the early 1970s the first British champion to be brought into the States was Ch. Beau of Kyratown, and his proud owner was Mrs. Walter M. Jeffords. Etive Copplestone Pu Zin Julier was not a British champion when he arrived in the United States, but he was later reexported to the land of his birth where he proceeded to gain his British title. The beautiful Ch. Ralshams Lovely Lady was lured away from her breeder, Barbara Lashmar, whose kennel became so well known in England for her intense quality bitches. Kitty Duff then bought Ch. Beaupres Likely Lad of Patrona from Elizabeth and Fiona Mirylees, who were responsible for a large number of exports from their Beaupres Kennel. Antonia Horn exported from her Belknap Kennel Ch. Belknap Kalafrana Caspar to Mrs. Walter Maynard. Caspar was a son of the highly influential British sire Ch. Shiarita Cassidy, a dog whose pedigree represents a concentration of intense linebreeding on Jean Eisenman's Caversham-based Jamestown line. Ch. Micklee Ru's Romayo came out to Richard Hammond and Robert Jacobson, a rare import in that Mr. and Mrs. Jack Mitchell are known for not parting with their British champions. Ch. Rosayleen the Gaffer at Sunsalve had also been imported by Don Sutton and Dr. Steve Keating.

Two further British champions to journey across the Atlantic hailed from the relatively young Josto Kennel of Joan Stokoe. She sold Ch. Josto Royal Flush, to whom I awarded one of his earliest Challenge Certificates, to Michael Wolf, who subsequently sold him to Japan. He was followed by Ch. Josto Call Me Madame who went to the Pierrot's Kennel, for whom she became a useful producer.

Interestingly, it is not necessarily the British champions who have had the greatest impact on arrival in the States. One must bear in mind that many of the more significant dogs were bought before they had reached full maturity, and on the British show bench they would have been competing with the established, more "finished" champions of the day. For example, dogs of the caliber of Mandarin, Rikki, Chik T'sun and Dragon were bought before they had the opportunity to be seen as mature adults in their home country, yet their influence on the breed in the States is beyond question.

Further examples spring to mind: John Royce's Ch. Kai Jin of Caversham had a record second to none, and his value as a stud was put to great advantage by his sensible owner. Many of his homebred winners stemmed from this important stud dog. Dorothy Quigley's Ch. Kai Lung of Vinedeans is another such male.

Let us not forget that not all imports to this country have been rigidly campaigned or been backed by high-powered advertising. Even so, they have

Hope Hartenbach's Ch. Hope's Firecracker Sparkler is three generations of Hope's breeding on his dam's side.

A charming photograph of Hope Hartenbach (right) with a brace of Hope's champions and Brenda Scheiblauer with Ch. Hope's Mr. Sandman of Magic Charms and the English-born Pekehuis Masterpiece.

often been recognized as having virtues to offer and been utilized by intelligent breeders, and consequently made their contribution to the modern Pekingese.

By the middle of the twentieth century there existed in America a wide gene pool of Pekingese, imported and American-bred, and a number of dedicated owners and breeders. Alongside the lower-key breeders were to be found fanciers of the breed who had enormous enthusiasm—often with bank balances to match. While such supporters of a breed frequently prompt criticism from certain quarters, their contributions should not be undermined. Being prepared to finance the campaigning of outstanding dogs means that such animals get to be seen by a much larger viewing public than would normally be possible in a country as vast as ours. The more breeders who get to see the cream, the more likelihood they are to utilize them in an attempt to perpetuate their virtues. So let us not castigate the well-situated fanciers, for without them the progress of the modern Pekingese in America may well have moved along much more slowly.

Hope Hartenbach (Hope's)

Situated in Missouri is the Hope's Kennel of Hope Hartenbach, whose fascination for the breed spans more than a quarter century. The kennel has been responsible for many champions, and in recent years her Ch. Hope's Firecracker Sparkler has won the admiration of many breed connoisseurs. On his dam's side he is three-generation Hope's breeding, while his sire is Ch. St. Aubrey Sunburst of Elsdon. Sparkler's sister, Ch. Hope's Sun Kiss of Dawn, was linebred to Ch. Rodari the Dragon at Lon-Du to breed her Ch. Hope's Ko Ko Puff Dragon, the multiple Group winner. Mrs. Hartenbach's enthusiasm for the breed is an example to us all. Her frequent visits to Britain have ensured that she keeps abreast of the developments within the breed's adopted homeland, and her interest today is as acute as ever.

Mrs. Walter M. Jeffords (Chinatown)

Mrs. Walter M. Jeffords's kennel is probably the numerically largest Pekingese establishment in the United States today. Prior to succumbing to the fatal fascination of the Pekingese, Mrs. Jeffords more than made her mark in another difficult breed, the Boston Terrier. Turning her attentions to the Lion Dog of Peking some twenty years ago, Mrs. Jeffords's earliest winners were co-owned and handled by Michael Wolf. They constituted a formidable duo, amassing Bests in Show with their strong team. Many dogs were imported from Britain where she was a frequent visitor, always on the lookout for an ascendant star. Among her best-known winning dogs were Ch. Dagbury of Calartha, the English-imported Ch. Beau of Kyratown and Ch. Quikin the Stringman (twice winner of the Pekingese Club of America Specialty). Situated among the rolling countryside of Pennsylvania, the kennel building itself is a breeder's dream; large, bright and airy with every convenience for the residents. Since relinquishing her partnership with Mr. Wolf, Mrs. Jeffords has taken on the Chinatown

Few Pekingese live in such luxury as this group, some of Mrs. Walter M. Jeffords's "kennel" seen with their owner in her New York home.

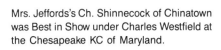

Mrs. Jeffords's Ch. Shinnecock of Chinatown was Best in Show under Charles Westfield at the Chesapeake KC of Maryland.

Ch. Chico of Chinatown winning Best in Show at the Pekingese Club of America under Michael Hill; handled by Hernan Martinez.

affix (which was at one time registered in England where, years ago, it was carried by many champions). Under the auspices of Mrs. Jeffords, the new American Chinatown will doubtless become equally famous. Indeed, in the past few years Mrs. Jeffords's breeding program has produced several top winners that have rocketed her to the forefront of the breed in America. Ch. Randolph, Ch. Shinnecock and Ch. Eskimo have all been Best in Show winners, while others such as Ch. Chico have scored well at Speciality events. Chico took Best at the Pekingese Club of America Specialty for American-breds in 1987, then the following year it was won by Shinnecock. Mrs. Jeffords's homebred stock stems from a variety of imports she secured over the years.

Edward B. Jenner (Knolland Farm)

Few people have had the numbers of outstanding Pekingese that Edward B. Jenner has been privileged to own. A connoisseur of livestock in general for many years, Mr. Jenner's involvement with the Pekingese breed stems from the mid-sixties. Ch. Colden Jasper O'Dene Shay, an English import, was one of his earliest big winners. He later acquired Ch. St. Aubrey Singlewell T'Sae Wen in 1973. A contemporary of Jasper O'Dene Shay's at Mr. Jenner's Knolland Kennel was his other British import, Ch. Etive Copplestone Pu Zin Julier. At this time Mr. Jenner's dogs were being handled by Edna Voyles, and she felt that Jasper was a better prospect than Julier and so persuaded her client to let Julier return to England to his former owner, Diana Holman. What a wonderful stroke of fate that decision turned out to be, for when Julier returned to Britain he was used by Lilian Snook on her Laparata Celeste to produce her first champion, Laparata Celestial Star. This breeding represented the crème de la crème of British Pekingese breeding since Julier traced back on the tail male line through four generations of champions to Ch. Caversham Ku Ku of Yam, while Celeste went back to Ku Ku through Ch. Ku Jin of Caversham, Ch. Goofus Le Grisbie and Ch. Yu Yang of Jamestown. Mrs. Snook had produced a bitch, Laparata Miranda, by breeding Celeste to her own Laparata François. He was a grandson of Laparata Gay Sir, full brother to Celeste, to whom he was subsequently mated. When Miranda and Celestial Star were bred, a dog puppy called Laparata Dragon was the result, and considering the foregoing, was it really surprising that the Mighty Dragon was to make such an immeasurable contribution to the modern Pekingese in America?

Dragon was first introduced to me by Mrs. Snook, his breeder, at a London Pekingese Club show when he was nine months old. He was not the slightest bit impressed, yet to say that I was impressed by him is a gross understatement. The more I studied this unknown young dog's attributes, the more convinced I became that he impressed me more than any other I had seen in many a year. He was fascinating to look at—intense in his quality, exciting in his type, illustrious in his background and challengingly independent in his demeanor. This dog presented a challenge, and I had to have him! Like most beautiful dogs, Dragon seemed to know how handsome he was, and with typical Pekingese character he left me in no doubt that he didn't give a damn for me or any other mere mortal. After a lapse of several years, I felt again the excitement I had experienced when stumbling across the young Chik T'Sun, Mandarin and Rikki, and bearing in mind that the longer one is involved with a breed, the more discerning one becomes, I figured that the young Dragon was likely to be an even greater prospect. This independent, arrogant beast was as charismatic and aloof as his imperial ancestors, and I knew that I had to have him.

His behavior in the ring was stubborn, uncompromising and totally Pekingese. The encouragement of toys and tidbits were beneath him. He was a great Pekingese; such offerings were an insult. For him the comforts of his show basket, not the rigors of the show ring, made for greater sense. The more he resisted, the more appealing he became. I wanted him. Mrs. Snook didn't want to sell. It was a Wednesday night; in retrospect, it was probably one of the longest nights of my life. There were calls to Mrs. Snook and almost as many calls to my partner Bill. He had not witnessed the dog in person. All he was interested in was this magical pedigree, the result of a half-brother to half-sister breeding on superbly bred Pekingese, a mating that has always instilled confidence. Since Dragon's double granddam, Celeste, was a daughter of Ch. Cherangani Chips, Bill was even more enthusiastic because Chips had been his Best of Breed winner at the third championship show he judged in England, and in his eyes Chips was a special dog.

Wednesday through Sunday passed slowly, but eventually I persuaded Mrs. Snook that Dragon's future lay in the United States, and on the following Tuesday he accompanied me home. Thus the first stages in a turning point in modern Pekingese history had begun. I shall return to the Dragon in a while.

Meantime, Ed Jenner had obtained several quality Pekingese that his handler, Luc Boileau, had campaigned for him, and Knolland Farm was becoming well known for its interest in the breed.

Dragon lived with us—or, to be more exact, we lived with Dragon—for a year in Canada. His show career was limited; his true value to us was fulfilling the role of stud dog, and happily we had available to us several bitches who complemented both his physique and his pedigree.

Very swiftly it became apparent that my faith in the reluctant hero had been justified. In Dragon we had obtained a prepotent stud dog who consistently produced compact, thickset bodies with very high tail sets (an important virtue that still comes through), coupled with his wide, shallow, glamorous face and coat properties. Despite his services being limited at that time to our own relatively small kennel, the Dragon's influence was definite and rapid.

For the Dragon, his new life-style at St. Aubrey was much to his liking. The reticent teenager soon developed into a mature stallion, strutting about his harem with confidence, style and great self-possession. He was blossoming as we could only have dreamed he would. After the champagne honeymoon at St. Aubrey-Elsdon it was agreed that he should go to Ed Jenner to be campaigned by his handler, Luc Boileau, and make as great a contribution to the modern American Pekingese as was possible. As a show dog he amassed some forty-two Bests

Ch. St. Aubrey Yorklee Fanfare Royale was imported from Britain, a grandson of two different sons of Ch. Yu Yang of Jamestown. Mated to the all-English-bred Can. Ch. Tiara of St. Aubrey Elsdon, he produced St. Aubrey Pendant of Elsdon, an excellent producer.

Am. & Can. Ch. St. Aubrey Laparata Dragon, a legendary stud force in contemporary American Pekingese history, was imported by Nigel Aubrey-Jones and R. William Taylor and later owned by Edward B. Jenner.

Am. & Can. Ch. St. Aubrey Dragonora of Elsdon was the top-winning Pekingese bitch of all time in the United States. Owned by Ann Snelling and bred by R. William Taylor, Dragonora was sired by Dragon out of the British import Can. Ch. St. Aubrey Knostro Sandrine. Her litter brother was the important stud dog Can. Ch. St. Aubrey Dragonfly of Elsdon.

The famous Ch. St. Aubrey Bees Wing of Elsdon, owned by Edward B. Jenner. Bees Wing was sired by Dragon out of his own granddaughter, Can. Ch. St. Aubrey Honeybee of Elsdon, which was by Dragonfly out of Pendant.

in Show, but when talking of Dragon, his show ring successes pale in significance against the contribution he made as a producer—and that, after all is said and done, was the reason I wanted him so desperately.

Of the many children of note to come directly from Dragon, the two most famous without doubt were Ch. St. Aubrey Dragonora of Elsdon (from a direct British imported bitch) and Ch. St. Aubrey Bees Wing of Elsdon. Ch. St. Aubrey Dragonora was the top-winning Pekingese bitch of all time, whose show career climaxed with Best in Show at Westminster when in the ownership of Anne Snelling and handled by William Trainor. It is the opinion of my partner and me that this wondrously typical bitch is one of the best bitches we have ever bred. The second of Dragon's most illustrious get, Ch. St. Aubrey Bees Wing of Elsdon, was owned by Mr. Jenner and piloted by Luc Boileau, for whom he won some thirty-seven Bests in Show as well as the Quaker Oats Award and Top Toy Dog. Three years in succession Bees Wing won the Pekingese Club of America Summer Specialty, and he has, in turn, proved to be a sire of some consequence.

As we look at the success of further Pekingese kennels of the present day, the far-reaching effects of the Dragon will manifest themselves further. For me, "chasing the Dragon" proved one of the most rewarding experiences of a lifetime devoted to this breed. He was that rare animal, a legend in his own lifetime. He provided a link with the past that paved the way to the future. He was, in all senses of the word, a great Pekingese.

Mr. Jenner's enthusiasm for the breed had resulted in his obtaining such dogs as Am. & Can. Ch. Temple Bells of Blossomlea, which I had campaigned in Canada before letting him come to the States. A son of Goofus Fangio Tu, the English import by Ch. Goofus Le Grisbie, Temple Bells was a multiple Group winner handled by Elaine Rigden for Ed Jenner. Later came the British import, Ch. St. Aubrey Pai Foo of Wychstock, which made a great contribution as a stud dog and also made his presence acutely felt in the show ring. Another English dog to grace Knolland Farm was Ch. St. Aubrey Lisret Twee Jin T'sun, which brought a significantly Caversham heritage. Mr. Jenner also had Ch. Changte San Sable, bred in Pauline Bull's famous English kennel and sired by Ch. Tsungli San Fou of Changte, an important British stud of the time.

Then enter the Dragon! Apart from owning the great dog himself, Mr. Jenner campaigned the homebred Ch. Knolland Tiger Rag, a multiple Group and Best in Show winner, a Dragon son; Ch. St. Aubrey Romany of Elsdon, a Dragon grandson through his son Can. Ch. St. Aubrey Dragonfly of Elsdon, which won the breed at Westminster before returning to Canada where he was actively campaigned, still in Mr. Jenner's ownership, to win Best Toy Dog of the year; Ch. St. Aubrey Bees Wing of Elsdon, by Dragon out of his own granddaughter through Dragonfly, which went on to win the Ken-L Ration award for Top Toy Dog in the United States during 1986, taking the breed at Westminster the following year. Bees Wing has proved to be a more than worthy stud dog, as his ancestry suggested he might.

Am. & Can. Ch. St. Aubrey Ladybird of Elsdon was a daughter of Mayfly out of Can. Ch. St. Aubrey Ladybug, also by Dragon and sister to Honeybee, the dam of Bees Wing. She is seen being handled by her owner-breeder R. William Taylor to win Best of Winners at the Pekingese Club of America 1984 Summer Specialty under Mrs. James Edward Clark.

One of Edward B. Jenner's many British imports, Ch. Changte San Sable, pictured here winning Best of Breed at Westminster under Sari Brewster Tietjen and being handled by Luc Boileau.

The culmination of many years of dedication to Pekingese came for Mr. Jenner when his Ch. Wendessa Crown Prince took Best in Show at Westminster in 1990, a poignant and fitting win in many ways because it marked the retirement of Luc Boileau as Mr. Jenner's handler, his having previously made the decision to begin judging. Happily for the breed, Mr. Boileau and Mr. Jenner will continue to co-own a select team of dogs that will be exhibited when circumstances allow.

Crown Prince is walking proof of the wisdom of combining linebred prepotent male lines with outcross bitches, and his pedigree bears close analysis. Interestingly, and as credit to the archivists who have documented the breed so carefully, elsewhere in this book appears a chart that traces Crown Prince, in tail male line, right back to Ah Cum, one of the original Pekingese snatched from the Imperial Palace one hundred years ago.

Crown Prince's sire was Ch. Briarcourt's Rule Britannia, produced by breeding an Australian imported bitch to Am. & Can. Ch. St. Aubrey Sunburst of Elsdon, whose parents were both by Dragon out of two different English imported bitches.

Crown Prince's dam, Ch. Wendessa Princess Lyzette, however, was the result of mating Dragon to his own granddaughter, Ch. Lady Farrah of Fourwinds, whose sire was an unrelated English import.

Breeding Lyzette to Britannia produced a pedigree that contained four lines to Dragon in as many generations as well as valuable outcrosses. His success at Westminster brought valuable publicity for the breed, and in the eyes of the cognoscente the win was all the sweeter in view of the fact that Best in Show was judged by Frank Sabella, one-time handler of such wonderful Pekingese as Ch. Calartha Mandarin of Jehol.

Coincidentally, Rule Britannia's paternal grandsire, Can. Ch. St. Aubrey Dragonfly of Elsdon, was a litter brother to Dragonora, the last Pekingese to win the Garden. Dragonfly was shown only twice in the States and never returned to claim his crown, yet it is my and my partner's contention that he is one of our most outstanding males and a stud dog of great worth.

In a country as widespread as the United States, there are many strongholds within the Pekingese fancy, and from area to area type may vary a little, just as it would in smaller countries within the same proximity. The fact that there exist so many subtle variations on the theme of the breed Standard is not necessarily a bad thing, for it gives breeders wells on which to draw when they feel the need to improve specific breed points within their own kennels.

Not wishing to turn this work into an elaborate show catalog, I have attempted below to give a cross section of other present-day Pekingese fanciers whose activities as breeders and/or exhibitors have contributed to the profile of the modern Pekingese in America.

It would be pointless to separate the United States and Canada where the contemporary Pekingese scene is concerned because there is such cooperation between the two countries, with much interaction between breeders and kennels.

Lingling Gypsy Sue was imported from Australia by R. William Taylor and won her title in both Canada and the United States where she was a group winner. She is pictured being handled by Nigel Aubrey-Jones to win a Group under the famous British judge, the late Stanley Dangerfield.

Am. & Can. Ch. St. Aubrey Romany of Elsdon, a son of Gypsy Sue and Dragonfly, seen winning under Shirley Limoges; handled by Nigel Aubrey-Jones. Bred by R. William Taylor, Romany is now the property of Carol Hollands.

Michael Hill (Akarana)

Of today's Canadian Pekingese fanciers, one of the keenest has to be Michael Hill of the Akarana Kennel. When living in his native New Zealand, Mr. Hill's parents were Shetland Sheepdog exhibitors, and it was here that he acquired his first Pekingese, a black granddaughter of the British champion Goofus Le Grisbie and Tul Tuo of Alderbourne. Going to live in Canada in the early 1970s, Mr. Hill's first champion was Can. Ch. Mandragora Fu Amity, a Best in Show winner with several Groups to her credit. The acquisition of two Ho Dynasty bitches brought Akarana firmly to the forefront. Ch. Akarana Silver Jubilee, a Group-winning black bitch, produced but one litter, sired by Can. Ch. St. Aubrey Dragon Boi of Elsdon, yet this contained Ch. Akarana Silver Fili-gree, a black bitch, and the well-known Am. & Can. Ch. Akarana the Aggressor—or "Butch." Butch won his first Best in Show at just ten months of age, and by one year he had won four more. At the time of his comparatively early retirement, he had won thirty Group firsts, ten Bests in Show, plus two Specialty Bests in Canada as well as a Specialty Best and several Group firsts in the United States. He was Canada's Top Toy Dog in 1980 and number one Pekingese in 1980 and 1982. Am. & Can. Ch. Ho Dynasty's Chantilly, a multiple Group winner, was bred to the sire of the Aggressor, Ch. St. Aubrey Dragon Boi of Elsdon, to produce one Group-winning daughter, Ch. Akarana Victorian Lace.

The mating of these Ho Dynasty bitches to Ch. St. Aubrey Dragon Boi of Elsdon gave Akarana a solid foundation, and it is interesting to note that Ho Dynasty carries heavy lineage to the famous father and son, Mandarin and Rikki, imported by St. Aubrey-Elsdon, and further descends from Ch. Simba Sal of Elsdon, the first champion to be bred by R. William Taylor.

The Aggressor is the sire or grandsire of many excellent winning progeny on both sides of the border. Victorian Lace by Ch. St. Aubrey Dragon Boi of Elsdon has subsequently produced six champion children, four of them Toy Group winners.

Of interest is the fact that Best of Breed winners at the 1986 and 1987 Pekin Palace Dog Association (Canada) Specialty Shows were litter brother and sister Ch. Akarana Tony Gable and Ch. Akarana Gable Lace, owned by John and Beth Ferrier. These siblings were sired by Ch. St. Aubrey Yu Tong of Elsdon out of a daughter of Ch. Akarana the Aggressor and Ch. Akarana Victorian Lace. This daughter is a result of a half brother and sister mating, the common grand-sire being Ch. St. Aubrey Dragon Boi of Elsdon.

Audrey A. Atherton (Audrianne)

Few fanciers have shown such unswerving loyalty to the breed over many years as has Audrey A. Atherton of Ohio. Her Audrianne Kennel has housed over thirty champions, and she has always taken a special interest in the white Pekingese, arguably the most difficult color to breed.

Michael Hill's Am. & Can. Akarana the Aggressor, owner-bred from Ch. Akarana Silver Jubilee and Ch. St. Aubrey Dragon Boi of Elsdon, which was by Dragon out of Dragon's half sister.

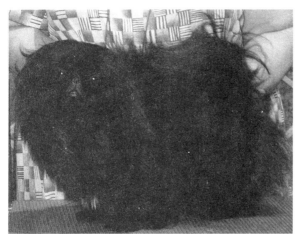

Ch. Audrianne's Midnight Magic, a granddaughter of Am. & Can. Ch. Shady Acre's Tux's Sambeau, as owner-handled to her title by Audrey A. Atherton.

Miss Atherton has always taken a special interest in white Pekingese. Here is one of her champions, a daughter of two British imports, Ch. Hyldewood Loofoo Snow Sprite and Beaupres Snow Shani.

40

Reg and Flora Crane (Polina)

In Canada's easternmost province, Newfoundland, resides the Polina Kennels of Reg and Flora Crane, the name Polina deriving from a famous whaling ship immortalized in an old Newfoundland folk song. Canadian stock that incorporated English bloodlines founded the kennel in 1964, but after 1973 when the Cranes first visited Crufts, a succession of British imports followed across the North Atlantic, mainly from the Penang Kennels of Mr. and Mrs. J. Simpson. They included Penang Fu O'Fire, Sankirk Susi of Penang, Penang Wonderwoman, Penang the Whistler and Penang Judy Blum, all of which became champions in their adopted country. Ch. Belknap Pockets Pasha and Kintoo Posy of Belknap came from Antonia Horn's Belknap Kennel in Dorset. All these imports made great contributions to the Polina breeding program.

More recently the Polinas have returned to their roots, and their most recent winners have been Canadian-bred, either homebred or from the St. Aubrey-Elsdon Kennels. Their record holder is the Best in Show winner Ch. St. Aubrey Royal of Elsdon, sired by the English-bred Laparata Royalty at St. Aubrey out of Ch. St. Aubrey Honey Bee of Elsdon, a daughter of Ch. St. Aubrey Dragonfly of Elsdon. As well as having a dazzling show career, Royal has produced to date four champions, with others on their way to titles.

Due to their location, the Polina Kennels do not have easy access to top stud dogs or a great number of shows, yet no less than thirty-four champions have been made up by the kennels, twenty of which bear the Polina name.

Bill and Elaine Bergum (Ber-Gum)

Early in 1990 I heard of the sad passing of Elaine Bergum who, with her husband, William, ran a small fancier's kennel in California. The Bergums kept Pekingese primarily for pleasure and the enjoyment that results from sharing one's home with such a charming and intelligent breed, yet their show ring successes with the Ber-Gum Pekingese were many. The Bergums began breeding in the 1940s, yet the late Mrs. Bergum had been introduced to the breed much earlier: her parents had bought her a pet Pekingese when she was just six years old. Mrs. Bergum's mother, not surprisingly, became fascinated by the breed and soon began breeding Pekingese under the Ragland affix. Shortly after Bill and Elaine were married, the gift of a Ragland bitch arrived, and so the Ber-Gum Pekingese were born.

Always owner-handled, the Ber-Gum Pekingese were strongly represented in the "Bred by Exhibitor" class, and Ch. Ber-Gum's Dee Oh Gee, a multiple Group winner, took one of his Groups from this very class. Ch. Choo Lin of Ber-Gum was a Best in Show winner while other Group winners bred by the Bergums included Ch. Trini Lo of Ber-Gum, Ch. Ti Ja of Ber-Gum, Ch. Koko Puff of Ber-Gum, Ch. Topaz Lin of Ber-Gum and Ch. Ber-Gum's China Sam, with Topaz becoming the top-winning bitch in her area. She won and placed in many Groups, winning both the Arizona and Southern California Specialties.

Can. Ch. St. Aubrey Royal of Elsdon, owned by Mr. and Mrs. Reg Crane. Bred by R. William Taylor.

The late Elaine Bergum's Ch. Ber-Gum's Tui Flower.

Ch. Saki of Del Sol, a beautiful cream bitch that won well for Mr. and Mrs. William Bergum in the 1960s.

43

Christine Hann (Chambrae)

As a young girl, Christine Hann had longed for a Pekingese of her own, but she had to wait until she was married in 1966 to fulfill that childhood dream. Her first Pekingese was a parti-colored bitch of Caversham and Coronation lines that was eventually bred to her grandsire, Ch. Coronation T'Sun Shee, and produced one bitch puppy. Mother and daughter became the foundation of Christine's Chambrae Kennel. Answering an advertisement for show-quality Pekingese puppies, Christine bought a son of Ch. Cho-Sen's Robin of Pierot that she discovered was a monorchid—at their first show! He was replaced with a male from the same kennel that cost four times the price of his incomplete predecessor. This dog puppy, Kentucky Colonel Aristocrat, was Christine's first show dog, and together they learned the ropes. He won a Toy Group in 1973 under Mrs. James Edward Clark, but his owner's proudest moment came when, from the Veterans Class, he took Best in Show at the North Central Illinois Pekingese Club Specialty. He produced five champions, four for his home kennel.

In 1968, Christine brought in from England a fawn bitch called Changkim Moon Princess that became her second owner-handled champion. She was followed by another Changkim import, Moon Dust, but she came from Australia, where Mr. and Mrs. Pearson had relocated their Changkim Kennel. From her came the top-winning black bitch Ch. Black Tia of Chambrae. Using this stock as her foundation, after some twenty years in the breed, Christine has bred twelve champions, ten of them breeder-owner-handled, and finished a total of fifteen champions. Like so many who form the "backbone" of this breed, Christine prefers to maintain a small, select kennel of dogs that are owner-handled, thus preserving a personal relationship with her Pekingese.

Anna M. Stephens (Cheri-Li)

Now retired from judging and exhibiting, but still under the spell of Pekingese as companions, is Anna M. Stephens, whose Cheri-Li Kennel dates back to the early 1940s and whose exhibiting began in 1948. An early import from Great Britain was the Irish-bred Deliah of Colindene. In over forty years of breeding and showing, Anna has developed a distinctive line of Pekingese and a sound philosophy that has resulted in many champions. She finished Choo Cee of Margle, and later acquired Ch. Sand Man of Honan. These two first champions were bred together to produce Ch. Cho Sen Mona Lisa, the first homebred champion for the Cho Sen Kennel.

Jerry and Edna Voyles (Cho Sen)

While in Canada showing Sand Man and his daughter Mona Lisa, Jerry and Edna Voyles, met Ted Ward (father of the renowned terrier handler, George), who introduced them to the English import Wardene Sun Fo. It was love at first sight, and Sun Fo returned home to become part of the Voyles's household. He

R. William Taylor awarding a Specialty Best of Breed to Ch. Black Tia of Chambrae, owner-handled by Christine L. Hann.

The Cheri-Li Kennel of Anna M. Stephens dates back to the 1940s. Pictured is her Am. & Can. Ch. Sing Lee Tom-Mi T'Sun of Cheri Li that was bred by Irene Ruschhaupt in California. The judge is Mrs. Schroeder Welsh.

finished fast, was used on Choo Cee with success, and complementing these lines with outcrosses from the Jalna and Dah Lyn lines, Cho Sen soon became a force to be reckoned with. Mrs. Voyles did well from the purchase of St. Aubrey Mayfly of Allinvale, and she also imported from Belgium Ch. Chik Tu of Pepperstiche who completed his American championship in seventy-two hours! An additional import to Cho Sen was the English male Ch. Jamestown Kan Jin of Caversham, and other English dogs followed, such as Etive Augusta Uncle Max and Knostro Lord Marcus of Etive.

Mrs. Voyles has always enjoyed the support of her husband, Jerry, who observes dryly, "I know there's money in dogs . . . I've been putting it there for years!"

Patricia and Charles Farley (Chu Lai)

More than twenty years ago Patricia and Charles Farley of Massachusetts bought their first Pekingese. He was a tricolor and spawned a great love for the breed. The Farleys' first bitch arrived in December 1970, became Ch. Chu Lai's Little Sissi Su and was duly bred to the original dog "Nikki." The first home-bred pup became Ch. Chu Lai Dan Dee Ting, which gained his title before his dam won her crown. Sissi Su was then bred to Michael Wolf's English-imported Ch. Bracewell Giacomo, produced two males by Caesarean section and died fourteen hours after whelping. Such tragedies often occur in the unpredictable world of dog breeding and sort the wheat from the chaff. No amount of setbacks will deter the Pekingese enthusiast who really loves the breed.

In the early 1970s the Farleys took advantage of the disbanding of Frances Kukla's Ding Ho Kennel, which had been based on Dah Lyn bloodlines, and they acquired several lovely bitches. Many champions have been finished by the Chu Lais, and in recent years the kennel has co-owned several Pekingese with Betty Whitford of the Pleiku Kennel. American-born Betty (then Mrs. Dupras) lived for several years in the United Kingdom where her husband was a U.S. serviceman. There she established a high-quality kennel based on Singlewell bloodlines, and she left behind her the white, Pleiku Snow Shan of Hyldewood, which was campaigned to his British title by Hylda Garwood. He was one of the very few whites to become a champion in the United Kingdom. The Farleys also pride themselves on owner-handling their dogs.

Mrs. Robert I. Ballinger, Jr. (Claymore)

Claymore is the kennel affix of Mrs. Robert I. Ballinger, Jr., of Florida, who has been breeding Pekingese since the early 1970s. Having produced her first homebred litter in 1971, Mrs. Ballinger journeyed to England the following year to visit the Crufts show in search of additional breeding stock. There she found a son of the prolific and dominant Ch. Yu Yang of Jamestown, Dorodea Yu Sam T'Sun, and a bitch of slightly similar lines, Volksmana Mi Queen.

Mrs. Ballinger breeds one or two litters each year, keeps a small select

Edna Voyles's Ch. Chik Tu of Pepperstiche completed his U.S. title in seventy-two hours. He was also a champion in Italy, Belgium, France and Monaco. Mrs. Voyles imported him from Baroness de Rudisch in Brussels, and he won several Group Firsts.

The last Pekingese to be imported and shown by Edna Voyles was the British-bred Ch. Knostro Lord Marcus of Etive.

Patricia and Charles Farley's first homebred puppy grew up to become Ch. Chu Lai Dan Dee Ting.

47

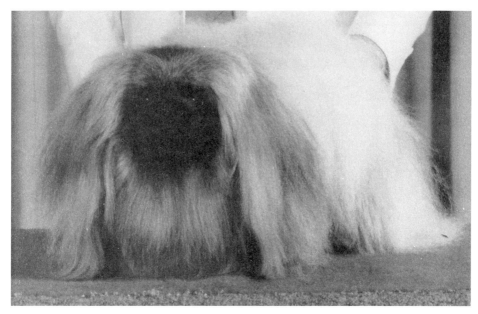

Ch. Chu Lai Touch of Buddha, a Toy Group winner, owner-bred by Patricia and Charles Farley and Frances Kukla.

Ch. Morningstar Lionheart, owned by Mrs. Robert I. Ballinger, Jr.

48

kennel and always handles her own dogs. She has finished many champions, with Ch. Claymore's Cinnamon Bun rising to number two Pekingese in the United States, having over fifty Group placings and three all-breed Bests in Show. One week after his third Best, this precious dog was operated on for an intestinal obstruction but did not survive. The loss was deeply felt by his devoted owner. Mrs. Ballinger did not give up, however, and campaigned further champions, but as her health declined she sold most of her dogs, including several who became champions in other hands. In 1977 the Ballingers moved to Florida where, happily, Mrs. Ballinger's health improved dramatically. In 1983 she returned to exhibiting with a Dragon grandson, Ch. Knolland Slowboat to China, which was actively campaigned. When bred to a Bees Wing daughter, this dog produced the twelfth homebred champion for Mrs. Ballinger in Ch. Claymore Four Leaf Clover.

A trip to England in 1985 saw Mrs. Ballinger returning with Toydom Accepts with Pleasure, a bitch, and Dratsum Captain Courageous, like the bitch sired by a Toydom champion. Both have acquitted themselves well in the show ring and breeding stakes. In 1986, Mrs. Ballinger finally managed to obtain an exceptional young dog she had wanted since the first time she saw him from his breeders, Anthony E. Rosato and John D. French. Ch. Morningstar Lionheart distinguished himself in the ring, always owner-handled.

Following the death of Mr. Ballinger, his widow returned to England in 1987 where she bought two young bitches that will doubtless play their part in the continuing story of the Claymores.

Hal Fraser and Allen Williams (Dragonhai)

Hal Fraser and Allen Williams were drawn into the Pekingese fancy about thirty years ago. As novices they found that American breeders were often reluctant to part with top-quality stock to beginners, and so they felt that corresponding with British breeders would prove more fruitful.

Their first import was Ch. Chi La Tu of Orchid Dell, which provided a sound foundation for the embryonic Dragonhai Kennel, followed afterward from Mary de Pledge by Ch. Shan-Jin of Caversham, which was to become the wellspring of the Dragonhai line. Through linebreeding to Caversham-bred stock the partners aimed to continue the Caversham line, a policy that several breeders on this side of the Atlantic had doubtless tried to adopt. Whether or not Miss de Pledge would have approved of their breeding programs is another matter.

From Diana Holman's Etive Kennel in England, the Dragonhai partners procured the top-winning puppy Ch. Etive Pu Yong, later to be joined by his cousin, Ch. Etive Ophelia.

The early days of Dragonhai saw Hal Fraser and Allen Williams actually finding their personal ideal in the Pekingese in the form of Ch. St. Aubrey Yen Lo of Sualane. The partners purport that of all the St. Aubrey imports, Yen Lo was one of the most overlooked and underappreciated. I daresay they may have a point. Yen Lo was certainly an impressive, handsome dog. A Yen Lo son went to Dragonhai, Ch. St. Aubrey Wee Yen of Church Road Farm, thus giving the kennel another source of Caversham concentrate.

In 1976 a family crisis demanded that the Dragonhai Kennel be disbanded. Stock was placed in various ownerships where their influence is being seen to this day. Ten years later, with family obligations fulfilled, Dragonhai became reactivated.

The born-again Dragonhai turned to New Zealand for its new foundations and secured from Hazel Rigden a Best in Show winner called N.Z. Ch. Regal Toff of Montresor. Needless to say, his ancestry is Caversham-based, and it was the hope of Fraser and Williams to combine his genetic heritage with that of some "recaptured" Dragonhai breeding, add some of the closely related Dragon blood and take up where they left off.

Mrs. Howard Eden Schultz (Eden Hill)

Mrs. Howard Eden Schultz began her obsession with the breed when her husband bought for her, as an anniversary present, "a fascinating red bundle of mystery." He was Mrs. Schultz's first dog, first Pekingese and first champion. A great-great-grandson of Ch. Chik T'Sun of Caversham, "Tang-Li" spurred on Mr. and Mrs. Schultz to find out more and more about the Pekingese breed. They became avid collectors of chinoiserie and received much help and encouragement from many stalwarts of the breed in their quest for additional quality specimens. Catherine Eadie Adam supplied Sam's Song of Tyneen, a British-bred son of the great British Ch. Redcoat of Kanghe, and Sam subsequently sired Ch. Sam T'Sun of Appin, the foundation stud dog at Eden Hill.

Having met Mrs. Gilma Blauvelt-Moss, Eden Hill acquired Ch. Ho Dynasty's Mor O'Mara, born in 1972, which established a fine winning record in the show ring but proved something of a disappointment in the whelping box. A bitch was brought in as a bride for Sam T'Sun, and their union brought about Ch. Play It Again Sam of Eden Hill. Ch. Yu Cherub's Dream of Appin was subsequently bred to their original Tang-Li, which gave the Schultzes the second homebred champion, Ch. Zinfidel of Eden Hill. The Eden Hill Pekingese are fortunate enough to live with their owners enfamille, so kennel life is something they will never have to experience.

Mr. and Mrs. Robert M. Jackson (Fourwinds)

Of today's American Pekingese exhibitors, few put more time and energy into their showing than Mr. and Mrs. Robert M. Jackson, whose Fourwinds Kennel has for many years been a force to be reckoned with. The first Pekingese was a Christmas present shortly after Mary Ann and Bob were married, back in the late 1940s. With a successful history of breeding sheep and cattle, it was a safe assumption that Bob Jackson would soon be breeding Pekingese, utilizing his experience and the knowledge of the importance of bloodlines and type in breeding.

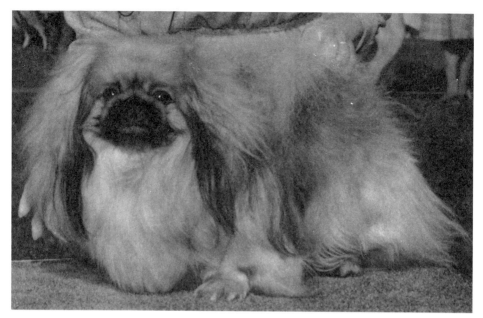

Mr. and Mrs. Howard Eden Schultz's Ch. Play It Again Sam of Eden Hill.

Ch. Zinfidel of Eden Hill, owned and bred by Mr. and Mrs. Howard Eden Schultz.

The Jacksons soon acknowledged that their first Pekingese was not the one on which they could build, so purchases were made from two of the leading kennels of the day, Orchard Hill and Dah-Lyn. This foundation stock enabled the Jacksons to produce their first homebred champions, Ch. Lu Jai Mee Too and Ch. Lu Tong Tu, both "of Fourwinds." Foundation bitches also included two granddaughters of the tragically lost British Ch. Yusen Yu Toi, one of them—Malita of Shades—becoming the Jacksons' first actual champion. When the Langridge Kennel was dispersed following its owner's death, three English-bred bitches were eagerly obtained, one being a daughter of British Ch. Ku Chi of Caversham, another being her daughter by British Ch. Tong Tuo of Alderbourne.

One of the important stud dogs of the time was Ch. Hi-Oasis of Brown's Den, which was entirely American-bred for four generations yet which quickly won his title in top competition. Another important sire for the Jacksons was Ch. Ki Yuki Ku of Wei Toi, which came to Fourwinds after the owners had seen him winning at Chicago. He was by the British import Ch. Caversham Khi Ku of Pendarvis, himself a son of the breed's blueprint, Ch. Caversham Ku Ku of Yam. Yuki sired several champions, doing especially well when Oasis daughters were bred to him. From such a mating came Ch. Khi Ku's Kin of Fourwinds, which sired quite a number of Fourwinds champions.

In the mid-sixties Merellen Manikin, a son of British Ch. Linsown Ku Che Tu, was imported from England. He won his title with all Group wins and took Best in Show the first time he was handled by Lorraine Heichel. His winning record gained momentum, and he sired over twenty champions, retiring from the show ring with twenty-three Group wins.

In 1974 the Jacksons traveled to England for the first time and were so impressed with the stock they saw that several more visits followed, each time the Jacksons bringing with them dogs whose type and bloodlines would complement the existing Fourwinds stock. Ch. Jamestown Jean's Dream was the first import, then came the black Ch. Singlewell Howz Dat, Ch. Toydom the Dramatist, Ch. Colhamdorn C'est Si Bon at Toydom (grandsire of the dam of Ch. Crown Prince, the 1990 Westminster Best in Show winner), Ch. Kalafrana Jay's Joseph at Toydom and Ch. Pendenrah Lysander of Sunsalve. These recent imports have given the Jacksons a kennel in which the majority of present inmates are linebred to the successful British sire Ch. Jay Trump of Sunsalve. More recently a son of another key British sire, Ch. Shiarita Cassidy, has been brought to Fourwinds: Ch. Mahjon Cassidy T'Sun. He has sired some fifteen champions, with his son, Ch. Fourwinds Cassius (sold to Ruby Dudley), siring almost as many.

Like so many, the Jacksons were quick to recognize the potential of Dragon, and they bred five champions from him, four from their excellent producing bitch, Ch. Violette of St. Aubrey-Elsdon.

Some 130 champions have been owned or sold by Fourwinds, and their strong kennel looks all set to figure in the Pekingese limelight for many years to come.

52

Mr. and Mrs. Robert M. Jackson's British-imported parti-color, Ch. Kalafrana Jay's Joseph at Toydom.

Mr. and Mrs. Robert M. Jackson's Ch. Fourwinds Flashin' Fashion.

Hetty Orringer (Hatamen)

Hetty Orringer's Hatamen Kennel is one of the smallest, housing but eight dogs, and is based on two litter sisters obtained from Edward Jenner's Knolland Farm Kennel, Ch. Knolland Noblesse Oblige and Morning Dancer. These sisters were bred to Ch. Laparata Celestial Prince and his distant cousin (also the sister's grandsire), Dragon, to produce a new generation of quality Pekingese whose Speciality wins are most creditable and that are in a position to ensure Hatamen is one of the names of the future.

Mr. and Mrs. George Hines (Hi-Trix)

When George Hines bought his wife, Mary, a Christmas gift of a Pekingese in 1981, little did he realize that he was sowing the seeds of an absorbing hobby that would survive the next decade! The Hineses' Hi-Trix Kennel bred their first champions when the specially bought foundation bitch was bred to Ch. St. Aubrey Yu Tong of Elsdon, their children including Ch. Hi-Trix Yu Tong Chopsticks and Ch. Hi-Trix Shanghi Queen, born in 1985. The base stock was augmented in 1984 with two more Yu Tong daughters from the Rodari Kennel in Canada. One of these was then bred to Ch. Briarcourt's Coral Gable to produce his first champion offspring, Ch. Hi-Trix Chia Pao.

In a relatively short space of time the Hineses have established a small kennel where the emphasis is on quality linebreeding. They would appear to be well set up for a rosy future in the breed of their choice.

Leo and Mary Jo O'Leary (Ho Toi)

The Ho Toi Pekingese of Leo and Mary Jo O'Leary came about in the mid-sixties when they obtained from Ruby Turner Williams a black-and-white parti-colored bitch, Top Hat's Pied Pixie of He'Lo. In her first litter to Puz Fondu of Dragonhai, Pixie produced the O'Leary's first champion, Pixie's Marmalade Kid of Ho Toi. In 1976 they bought Ch. Beverlyhill Saton's Sherrie of Se-Je in whelp to Mye Sun Chello, subsequently producing a litter that contained Ch. Sherrie's Samson of Ho Toi and Ch. Sherrie's Circe of Ho Toi. Circe went on to produce five champions, by Marmalade Kid, by a son of brother Samson and by an unrelated Dragon grandson.

Several of Ho Toi's champions have placed well in Groups, and the O'Learys are proud of having started the Colony Pekingese Club of the Southern Tier in 1981.

Arlon D. Duit (Lon-Du)

In Monticello, Iowa, will be found the Lon-Du Pekingese of Arlon D. Duit. Starting in 1975 with a pet male eight years old, the Duits were soon hit by the show bug, and within a year of entering their first dog show were showing

Ch. Knolland Noblesse Oblige, seen here, and her litter sister, Knolland Morning Dancer, provided the foundation for Hetty Orringer's Hatamen Pekingese.

Mr. and Mrs. George Hines's Ch. Hi-Trix Chia Pao, first champion sired by Ch. Briarcourt's Coral Gable, shown with Pam Campbell.

Leo and Mary Jo O'Leary's winning black, Ch. the Microdot of Ho Toi.

a black granddaughter of Ch. Pekehuis Twee's Dan Sun. This bitch failed to reproduce, but following the purchase of a brother and sister of Su-Con's and Beverlyhills breeding, the first homebred champion soon arrived as Ch. Mi Twee Jai-Kee of Lon-Du. He sired several champions including Ch. Mi Twee Anna of Lon-Du, which when bred to Ch. Black Cavalier of Chambrae, produced the first Lon-Du black champion, Ch. Mi Black Knight of Lon-Du.

Ch. Wild Rain Boi of Panora joined the Lon-Dus in 1977, a grandson of two key British champions of the day, Yu Yang of Jamestown and Copplestone Pu Zee. He has sired several champions, and a subsequent addition—the bitch Cambalu Lady Margo—proved a most valuable brood bitch. The utilization of dogs such as Ch. Mahjon Cassidy T'sun and Ch. Rodari the Dragon has enabled the Lon-Du Kennel to consistently produce champions, and the recent addition of Ch. Warcrest the American Gigolo, of Belknap and Shiarita lines, suggests that the Duits will be breeding interesting stock for some years to come.

Frank Tingley (Lyt-Ton)

In North Carolina can be found Frank Tingley's Lyt-Ton Pekingese. Although Mr. Tingley has been raising Pekingese for thirty years, the first fifteen or so were confined to the occasional pet litter. Having been invited to a dog show, his interest in the breed as a competition prospect was aroused, and for some time he studied Mrs. C. L. Jordan very closely. Mrs. Jordan was quite famous in her area, and since she was rather a secretive person, Mr. Tingley watched her grooming and presentation in the hope that he would pick up useful tips. Soon he was talking to every Pekingese breeder who would listen, thirsty for any information that would be dropped in his path. Ruthe W. Painter and Candy McCall were particularly helpful.

Jameson May Ray of Lyt-Ton was a beautiful dog of basically Jamestown breeding, and he became Mr. Tingley's first champion. A daughter of his, Ch. T'Zee of Lyt-Ton, was bred back to her sire to produce the excellent brood bitch Moonie Marie of Lyt-Ton, whose show career was prematurely ended due to an eye injury. When bred to Ch. Knolland Dream Maker, she produced Ch. Marie's Dream of Lyt-Ton, while her dam, T'Zee, was put to Mr. Tingley's top-producing male, Ch. St. Aubrey Yu Tong of Elsdon. This union produced Ch. Tel-Star Lyt-Ton, which has enjoyed a successful show career.

Anthony E. Rosato and John D. French (Morningstar)

The Morningstar Pekingese of Anthony E. Rosato and John D. French were established in Indiana in 1981, a good deal of study in the principles of genetics and the history of the breed having been employed before the first Morningstar litter was actually bred. After careful consideration of pedigrees of many of the best known and best producing dogs through the years, in both Britain and America, it was decided to base a breeding program on the St. Aubrey-Elsdon and Belknap bloodlines. It was also decided to exercise judicious

Ch. Rodari the Dragon at Lon Du.

Frank L. Tingley's Ch. Clark Telstar Lyt-Ton, a son of Ch. St. Aubrey Yu Tong of Elsdon.

linebreeding and strict selection as the means to the formation of a new blood-line.

Hence two granddaughters of Dragon were obtained, as well as their grand-mother, Ch. Violette of St. Aubrey-Elsdon, herself a granddaughter of Ch. St. Aubrey Carnival Music of Eastfield. One of the Dragon granddaughters was mated to Am. & Can. Ch. St. Aubrey Sunburst of Elsdon, a double Dragon grandson as well as being doubled on Carnival Music. This breeding produced a beautiful-headed, heavily coated red dog with black mask, excelling in facial detail and breed type—Morningstar Sun King—which became the kennel's best producing stud dog.

Sun King in turn sired multiple Group winner Ch. Morningstar Lionhart, owned by Mrs. Robert I. Ballinger, Jr., and Ch. Morningstar Frangelico, which is the product of a breeding that traces seven lines to Ch. St. Aubrey Laparata Dragon.

In the summer of 1984, Mr. Rosato and Mr. French relocated to Florida, bringing with them twenty-five Pekingese. Among these were Ch. Cambalu Wee Sed T'Ruffles (a glamorous bitch of Sungarth and Singlewell breeding) and Cambalu King Bee Morningstar (a grandson of the famous British Ch. Belknap El Dorado and son of the big-winning bitch Ch. Cambalu Sunburst, a half sister to Sun King, both being sired by the aforementioned Ch. St. Aubrey Sunburst of Elsdon).

Since the Morningstars have been in Miami, a good many litters have been bred, from which have emerged numerous winning dogs that have enjoyed many major successes particularly at Specialty events.

Betty Claire Peacock (Peacock)

Betty Claire Peacock of Arkansas was just four years old when her parents bought an Orchard Hill puppy, and since that time she has never been without Pekingese. Attending her first show in 1968, Mrs. Peacock met Jean Thomas of the Ai Kou Pekingese and was convinced that she also wanted to exhibit and breed Pekingese. With a husband in the military this was not practical at the time, but in 1978 Mrs. Peacock bought from Mrs. Thomas Ai Kou Bell Boi, which sired the Peacocks' first homebred champion, Ch. Peacock Pu Ying Pop-pit. Showing sparingly, Mrs. Peacock has finished eighteen Pekingese as well as having campaigned champions in Japanese Chins and Papillons.

Jean Carroll (Su-Con)

Jean Carroll's Su-Con Kennel derived its name from its owner's two daugh-ters, Susan and Constance, and although during its time in Pekingese the Su-Con Kennel has bred little more than thirty litters, the ratio of championships com-pleted to puppies bred is an impressive 64.3 percent. A friendship with Mrs. Brayton Prescott and her daughter Charleen helped stimulate Mrs. Carroll's

58

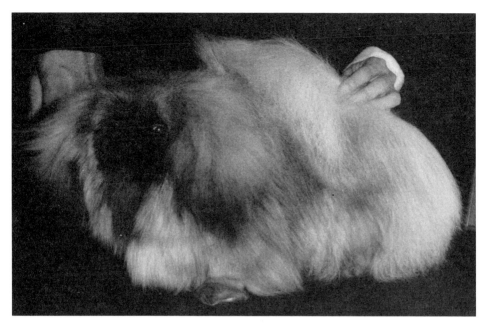

John French handled Morningstar Leonora, which he co-owns with co-breeder Anthony Rosato, to win Best Puppy under Terry Nethercott of the Sunsalve Pekingese in Great Britain. Leonora was sired by Ch. Morningstar Lionhart.

Jean Carroll's homebred Ch. Su-Con Color Me Special was a grandson of Ch. St. Aubrey Laparata Dragon and Ch. Pascan Picasso.

interest in the breed, and soon she was breeding and showing, and later obtained a professional handler's license, followed by a judge's license.

Am. & Can. Ch. Fu-Song's Half Note of Su-Con was the kennel's first Group-winning campaigner, and others soon followed. In a litter of four sired by Dragon, Su-Con produced four easy champions. More recently the English-imported bitch Changkim Tiff Annie was acquired with a view to augment the future breeding program.

Indeed, it was a Su-Con bitch, Rosetta, that provided the foundation for Karen Schultz's Sunburst Kennel. Breeding her to the British import Ch. Changkim Dallas of St. Aubrey seemed to Mrs. Schultz the perfect combination, and later she acquired British Ch. Changkim Moon River and her daughter Changkim Beach Candy to broaden the base of her kennel. Ch. Chan's Masked Marvel of Lyons joined Sunburst when Irene Reasons left for England, and although ten years old when arriving, he more than left his mark through his progeny. Breeding one of the Dallas/Rosetta daughters, Ch. Su-Con Drulette of Sunburst, to Ch. St. Aubrey Bees Wing of Elsdon gave Karen Schultz her current winner, the exquisite Ch. Sunburst Bees Whizz. Since Bees Wing is strongly linebred to Dragon, and Rosetta is a Dragon daughter, he should be an interesting prospect as a sire.

Patty Davis (V.I.P.)

The V.I.P. (Very Important Pekingese) Kennel of Patty Davis in California began when, after working with homeless dogs through the sixties, a Pekingese was bought from a pet shop. She was never bred, but soon two other bitches and a male were bought to provide a foundation for the kennel.

In 1977, Patty was given a black-and-white puppy by breeder Susan Medill, and she produced the first V.I.P.-bred champion, Ch. V.I.P.'s Parti Solo. It has long been Patty's ambition to produce superior parti-colors, an ambition she appears to be achieving.

Ruby Dudley (Dud-Lee)

Ruby Dudley's Dud-Lee Pekingese are Iowa-based and have been responsible for some one hundred champions, many of whom are behind, or have provided foundation stock for, other currently successful kennels. Mrs. Dudley's first big winner was a dog she purchased from the late Mrs. Adolph Ruschhaupt, Int. Ch. Ku Chin Tom-Mi of Seng Kye, the sire of seventeen champions. Other winners bred in the kennel included Am. & Can. Ch. Masterpiece Zodiac of Dud-Lee's who was successfully campaigned by Mrs. Dudley before he went to join Mrs. Walter Jeffords and Michael Wolf, in whose ownership he was piloted through to many top wins. Another memorable multiple Group winner was Ch. Dud-Lee's Khi Lyn's Masterpiece and, more recently, Ch. Dud-Lee's Lypton's Lysander.

Betty Claire Peacock's homebred Ch. Peacock the Sun in Splendor took a Best of Breed from the Puppy class.

Karen Schultz with Ch. Sunburst Bees Whizz winning one of many Specialty Bests in Show under Nigel Aubrey-Jones. He is a son of Ch. St. Aubrey Bees Wing of Elsdon.

When Jean Carroll bred her Su-Con Fortune Cookie to Ch. St. Aubrey Laparata Dragon, she produced four puppies, each of which became champions. One of the four, Ch. Su-Con Stoney Dragon, is pictured with handler Luc Boileau winning under Norman Patton.

The import, Ch. Changkim Dominic, was owned by Anna Engstrom, Mr. Lawson and Michael Sauve, who is seen handling him here. Mrs. Engstrom has bred several champions in her Eng's kennel.

Ch. Briarcourt's Coral Gable bred by Joan Mylchreest and campaigned by William McKay to an outstanding record during the mid-1980s. A Westminster Toy Group winner, this dog collected twenty-five Bests in Show, 107 Toy Group victories and seven Specialty Bests of Breed. Coral Gable is shown here with this handler David Fitzpatrick. *Kernan*

Sandy Wheat (Mugiechun)

The Mugiechun Pekingese of Sandy Wheat in Arizona constitute a small kennel, yet they are consistent winners of an identical type. Mrs. Wheat purchased the Mayfly daughter Ch. St. Aubrey Maydrena of Elsdon, followed by the Dragonfly son Ch. St. Aubrey Royal Star of Elsdon, and from them has developed a line of short, compact Pekingese of the highest quality. Her latest winner, Ch. Mugiechun Windy's Destiny, has experienced a most successful career to date.

Marjorie Kaye and Richard Kruger (Cambalu)

Marjorie Kaye and Richard Kruger own the Cambalu Pekingese in Missouri, and their breeding has long been in the forefront of producing dogs of exceptional qualities. Mrs. Kaye is an ardent student of pedigrees and believes that linebreeding to a type is the surest way to success. The kennel's top winner was the glamorous bitch Ch. Cambalu Hurly Burley, sired by Ch. Rodari the Dragon of Lon-Du, while their latest top-winning male is Ch. Cambalu Snapdragon, by the kennel's top producing Can. Ch. St. Aubrey Bumbee of Elsdon. Mrs. Kaye's and Mr. Kruger's obvious success is a result of breeding from their best bitches, and Cambalu has always had a strong hand in the distaff side.

Joan Mylchreest (Briarcourt's)

Joan Mylchreest is a shining example of someone who was not involved with the breed countless years before producing outstanding dogs. Her theory of buying the best available and then breeding to the best available producers has certainly paid dividends, for in the past few years she has bred in her kennel two of the breed's top winners: William McKay's Ch. Briarcourt's Coral Gable, a Group winner at Westminster, and Robert Jacobsen's Ch. Briarcourt's Excelsior. Coral Gable is the winner of twenty-five Bests in Show and 107 Group firsts, with seven Specialty Bests. Excelsior was a top California winner with twelve Bests in Show, sixty-nine Groups and three Specialty wins. However, perhaps Mrs. Mylchreest's greatest claim to fame is having bred Ch. Briarcourt's Rule Britannia, a phenomenal stud dog that produced not only the aforementioned two winners but also the 1990 Westminster Best in Show winner, Ch. Wendessa Crown Prince. Another multiple Group winner, with several Bests in Show to his credit, sired by Britannia, is Mr. Jacobsen's Ch. Muhlin Rob Roy of Mehling. Britannia was sired by the consistently good stud dog Am. & Can. Ch. St. Aubrey Sunburst of Elsdon out of one of Mrs. Mylchreest's several Australian imports. If Mrs. Mylchreest does nothing further in the breed, her name will go down in history as having given Pekingese an outstanding pillar of the breed in America.

Sandy Wheat handling her homebred Ch. Mugiechun's St. Aubrey Dragonwind, a son of Dragonfly and a highly successful stud dog, numbering among his winning offspring Ch. Mugiechun Windy's Destiny.

Ch. Cambalu Hurly Burly, a Group winner and a daughter of Ch. Rodari the Dragon of Lon Du and Ch. Cambalu Sunburst Crystal. Co-owner Richard Kruger is handling.

Ch. Cambalu Celestial Dragon, owned by Walt and Betsy Jones.

Duane Doll and Joe McGinnis (Elphasun)

In Florida the Elphasun Kennel of Duane Doll and Joe McGinnis has for some years been a force to be reckoned with. Their most famous resident was the lovely bitch Ch. Elphasun Arrhythmia, which became the breed's top-winning bitch of 1983 and 1984. The partnership also campaigned Ch. Sun Tai of the Gorge in co-ownership with Mrs. Fosella to win many Groups. He was also a Best in Show and Specialty Best winner. Doll and McGinnis have imported several Pekingese, the latest being the Welsh-bred Ch. Eirlyn Noel at Toydom, which quickly won his American championship.

Tom and Kathy Masilla (Santaverdi)

Tom and Kathy Masilla of New Orleans have brought their Santaverdi Kennel to prominence in recent times. Their current stars include the Best in Show winning Ch. St. Aubrey Jeeves of Elsdon, owned in partnership with Hiram Stewart, who handles him. Brenda Scheiblauer has handled Ch. Santaverdi the Wiseguy for them to many Group wins. He is a grandson of Ch. Hope's Firecracker Sparkler, which was campaigned so successfully for Hope Hartenbach by the same handler.

Joe Joly (Jo-Li's)

A small but nonetheless influential kennel is that of Joe Joly, whose Jo-Li's Pekingese can be found in Florida. Few kennels have the distinction of having bred two Best in Show winners in one litter, yet Mr. Joly achieved this with his Ch. Jo-Li Wind in the Willows and Ch. Jo-Li Virtuous Dragon. Willows was a multiple Group and Best in Show winner, and also took the breed at Westminster in 1989. During that year he also gave Crown Prince a run for Top Pekingese, eventually being Runner-Up to the 1990 Westminster Best in Show winner. Virtuous Dragon was campaigned for Edward Jenner to many Group wins as well as Bests in Show. Both these dogs were sired by the Dragon son Am. & Can. Ch. St. Aubrey Bees Wing of Elsdon, out of a good-producing Dud-Lee bitch.

Robert Jacobsen (Sing-Lee)

In California the Sing-Lee Kennel has been at the top of the breed for many, many years. Founded by Mr. and Mrs. Adolph Ruschhaupt, the kennel was bequeathed to Robert Jacobsen upon Mrs. Ruschhaupt's death, after which the kennel presented to the show scene some of the greatest California winners. Mr. Jacobsen and his partner Janet Allen are past masters in the art of presentation, their presentation always doing justice to the quality of dogs they consistently show. They rarely exhibit outside California and the surrounding area, yet the occasional forays to the East were not in vain. One of their very typical

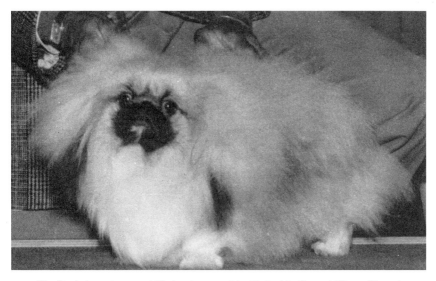

Ch. St. Aubrey Jeeves of Elsdon is owned by Kathy Masila and Hiram Stewart.

Ruthe W. Painter's Ch. Oakmere the Baron, imported from Olive Clay in England, was a Best in Show and multiple Group winner.

winners was the red Ch. Raffles Jubilation Sing Lee, which made the long journey to New York in 1984 to win Best in Show at the Pekingese Club of America Specialty for American-breds under Antonia Horn of the famous Belknap Kennel in England.

Winners followed upon winners, with some of their more prominent Best in Show and Group-winning Pekingese being Ch. Briarcourt's Excelsior, Ch. Muhlin Rob Roy of Mehling (both sired by Ch. Briarcourt Rule Britannia, Rob Roy being bred by Patty Mullendore and Diana Mehling). Recently Mr. Jacobsen's Specialty Best winners have included Ch. Windemere's Dragon Legacy, owned in partnership with his breeder Joy Thoms, and Ch. More Than a Dream at Katering, a son of Ch. Rodari the Dragon of Lon-Du.

Ruthe W. Painter (Panora)

Ruthe W. Painter's Panora Pekingese can be found outside Pittsburgh and have given the breed a considerable boost in that area. She has enjoyed great success with imported and American-bred stock alike, and not surprisingly many of her top winners were directly from Great Britain, a country she regularly visits. One of her first big winners was the United Kingdom import Ch. Oakmere the Baron, bred by Olive Clay, which was a Best in Show and multiple Group winner. Actively campaigned by Elaine Rigden, Baron became the top-winning Pekingese in the United States during 1975 and 1976. Mrs. Rigden also campaigned other imports for Mrs. Painter, such as Ch. Another Venture of Lotusgrange, a small, cobby red that did much to put the breed in the limelight, as did Ch. Pascan Picasso. Bred by Judith Risbey, this glamorous dog was a son of the eminent English stud dog Ch. Shiarita Cassidy.

Mrs. Painter's last big winner was the American-bred Ch. Ai Kou Master Chimes, which established an enviable winning record. With Mrs. Rigden's departure from handling, and joining the ranks of dog show judges, the Panoras have not been as active in the show ring as in the past, yet there is little doubt that with the enthusiasm of its owner, the kennel will continue to produce Pekingese of high quality.

Jean Thomas (Ai Kou)

The Ai Kou Kennel, based in Northern California and owned by Jean Thomas, produced numbers of stock of excellent quality. Sadly, Mrs. Thomas recently passed away, yet her efforts will, I feel sure, be continued by other dedicated breeders who have been fortunate enough to obtain her bloodlines. Mrs. Thomas's handler, Lois Frank, will retain an interest in the kennel and is continuing to show the typey young dog Ch. Ai Kou Weekend Warrior to many Specialty and Group wins. One of Mrs. Thomas's best homebreds was Ch. Ai Kou Sunni Dragon, a son of Dragon, which has inherited the ability to breed on and is already the sire of several champions.

Mrs. Thomas also imported a number of top specimens from Great Britain,

Elaine Rigden handling Ruthe W. Painter's Ch. Lotusgrange Another Venture, imported from his breeder, May Robertshaw, in England.

the most notable being Ch. Cherangani Bombardier that incorporates the line of the great British Ch. Cherangani Chips in his pedigree. He was a superb-headed dog, a feature he invariably transmitted to his progeny. Another top winner at "The House of Ai Kou" was the previously mentioned Ch. Ai Kou Master Chimes that had a short but meteoric career as a youngster before being sent east to continue his winning for Mrs. Painter.

John and Jay Thoms (Windemere)

In Oregon a long-established kennel with a reputation for breeding quality stock is the Windemeres of John and Jay Thoms. Their homebred winners have been numerous, but they have also been generous in allowing other breeders to obtain first-class specimens. The Thomses have also been at the helm in promoting the pure white variety, a difficult color in which to breed top quality and win. Citri White Wind was housed in their kennel and went on to sire several champions. In other colors, Ch. Windemere Sun Dragon, Ch. Windemere Magnum Force, Ch. Windemere Seeker of Fame, Ch. Windemere Hard to Be Humble and Ch. Windemere's Tanuki Tribute have all made their mark, adding to a long list of titleholders bred by the Thomses.

Dr. and Mrs. Ronald Bramson (Wendessa)

A decade is a short time for a kennel to be in existence, but to see such a young kennel produce a Best in Show winner at the most prestigious dog show in the United States is nothing short of miraculous. Dr. and Mrs. Bramson's Kennel in Maryland, Wendessa, did just that, but it would be quite wrong to assume that such a breeding was merely a lucky fluke. Indeed, it is hardly surprising if one has ever met and talked to Wendy Bramson, a lady who knew exactly what she wanted, was prepared to travel and see for herself before buying and was determined to obtain the very best available. Having flown to the Midwest to visit the Jacksons' Fourwinds Kennel, her heart was set on buying the best bitch she could find. She saw what she wanted and persuaded her owners to part with Lady Farrah of Fourwinds, by an English imported son of Ch. Jay Trump of Sunsalve out of a Dragon daughter. And the rest, as they say, is history. Farrah came out at the Pekingese Club Winner Specialty to win the sweepstakes under Candy McCall, then from the Puppy bitch class progressed right through to Best in Show under R. William Taylor. Farrah's fame did not stop there, however, for she quickly won her title, after which a litter was planned to the top-producing Ch. St. Aubrey Laparata Dragon, her maternal grandsire. From that breeding came the two champion sisters Ch. Wendessa Princess Lyzette and Ch. Wendessa London Bridgette, both of which won high awards at major events. Deciding to keep to the Dragon line, Lyzette was bred to Joan Mylchreest's Rule Britannia, and the result was Edward Jenner's Westminster 1990 Best in Show winner Ch. Wendessa Crown Prince.

Mrs. Walter Maynard's Ch. Velspring's Velvetina was actually bred in the United Kingdom but sired by Eng. & Am. Ch. Belknap Kalafrana Caspar before he left for the United States. She is seen here, handled by William Trainor, after winning a Group first under the popular young Finnish all-arounder, Rainer Vuorinen.

Patty Mullendore (Muhlin)

A number of kennels specialize in the smaller, compact Pekingese and consistently breed to type. One such is the Muhlin Kennel of Patty Mullendore, which has recently been associated with the establishment of Diana Mehling. They were basically founded on imported bloodlines, particularly Belknap. Mrs. Mullendore has always had a very strong attachment to the black Pekingese, a number of big winners having been bred in the kennel that lies behind some of the best-winning blacks in the country.

Mrs. Walter Maynard

Mrs. Walter Maynard's kennel on Long Island has never been a large establishment, and limited breeding has been of a selective nature. Her importation of Ch. Belknap Kalafrana Caspar, a son of Ch. Shiarita Cassidy, did a power of good for the breed, siring a dozen or so champions. His influence in other kennels was notable, particularly in the Chinatowns of Mrs. Walter Jeffords, for whom he sired Ch. Shinnecock, a Best in Show winner. Caspar was used at stud in England prior to his leaving for America, and it was there that he sired Velspring Velveteena, which was later to join her sire at Mrs. Maynard's Kennel. She immediately won well as a youngster, blossoming into a consistent winner of Groups and Bests in Show, handled by William Trainor. Two of her more notable wins were Best of Breed at the American Kennel Club's Centennial show under Geraldine Lee Hess, later taking Group Second, and Best of Breed at Westminster under Edward Jenner. Velveteena will go down in the history of the breed as one of the top show bitches of all time, her record being eclipsed only by the record Best in Show wins of Am. & Can. Ch. St. Aubrey Dragonora of Elsdon.

Peggy Dillard Carr

In the Tennessee-based kennel of Peggy Dillard Carr there was always to be found a dog worthy of hitting the high spots. Ch. St. Aubrey Kinwong Moon Shadow, Ch. St. Aubrey Chatterbox of Elsdon and Ch. St. Aubrey Yorklee Fanfare Royale followed one another in rapid succession as major contenders for Breed and Group wins.

Malcolm Moore and Dr. David Bowman

In Alabama can be found two enthusiastic supporters of the breed in Malcolm Moore and Dr. David Bowman. They campaigned Ch. Merrimac's Andreas Silbermann to many Best of Breed wins and Group placements, and more recently have concentrated on a British import, Ch. Etive Nutcracker.

Pamela Edmond, who owns the famous Singlewell Kennel in England, with one of her winners at the 1982 Pekingese Club of America Specialty, Mike Moore's Ch. Windemere's Blazing Dragon.

Am. & Can. Ch. Merrimac's Andreas Silbermann, the multiple breed winner, co-owned and breed by Malcolm Moore.

Annette L. Borders (Honeybear)

In Texas, Annette L. Borders's Honeybear Kennel can be depended on to bring out a homebred winner that will quickly gain championship honors in the keenest competition.

Mr. and Mrs. Schuerch (Paladin)

Mr. and Mrs. Schuerch's Paladin Kennel in western Pennsylvania is capable of breeding a top one. Their most famous winner is Ch. Paladin's Sneaky Pete, campaigned in partnership with Michael Wolf. He was Best in Show at the 1981 Pekingese Club of America Specialty show for American-breds under William Bergum.

Cleda Olsen (Shady Acre)

The Shady Acre Kennel of Cleda Olsen has always been a stronghold for the breed in the Midwest. A breeder of all colors, her fame will go down for producing spectacular parti-colors, while blacks have always played a large part in her breeding program. Her forays east to the Pekingese Club of America Specialty for American-breds only have proved more than successful. Indeed, her Ch. Shady Acres Tux's Sambeau won Best in Show in 1975 under Antonia Horn of the famous Belknaps in England. Again in 1979 the kennel took Best at this event under Geraldine Lee Hess with Ch. Shady Acres Beau-Smark.

Eva McMunn (Pierrot's)

In California one of the oldest and most respected kennels must be Pierrot's, founded by Eva McMunn in 1942 and now carried on by Mal and Lynn Simpson. The kennel imported the well-known English champion bitch Josto Call Me Madame, which gained her title in the States very quickly. She has also proved a good producer of champions, her titled progeny including Ch. Pierrot's China Raider and Ch. Pierrot's Wee Sed So.

Roger and Judy Sankey (Sanrae)

In Wisconsin, Roger and Judy Sankey have been building up their Sanrae Kennel by incorporating several bloodlines but concentrating more recently on the Dragon strain. Winners housed here included Ch. Muhlin Buckwheat of Mehling, Ch. Lou Shen's Ricochet and their recent Specialty winner, Ch. St. Aubrey Ruby of Elsdon, a daughter of Fr. & Can. Ch. St. Aubrey Jim Brady of Elsdon.

Larry Elks (Elksway)

Larry Elks is a keen supporter of the breed, being an enthusiastic student of pedigrees. His winners are a mixture of important bloodlines, and he has had much success in blending them. Ch. Pemyn Fanfare has been a recent import, as

74

was Ch. Changkim Mason Dixon. His Elksway Kennel in North Carolina has bred many winners including Ch. Elksway Entertainer (by Ch. Oakmere the Baron), Exclusive, Escort and Eyeful, to name just a few.

There would appear to be a healthy population of Pekingese breeders across the length and breadth of the United States who are well prepared for the nineties, with firm foundations on which to build dynasties of their own. The flood of British imports is perhaps now a trickle, and American-breds continue to hold their own at all levels of competition. That fact alone is a compliment to the American Pekingese breeders of the past and an encouragement to those of the future.

A British champion of the 1920s, Tai-Yang of Newnham, the breed's CC record holder to this day.

Ch. Copplestone Pu Zin, one of Yvonne Bentinck's famous champions, was an all-breed Best in Show winner. The Copplestone Kennel was destroyed in the late 1960s in a tragic fire.

Am. Ch. Chintoi Choir Boy, a white bred by Ella Pilgrim and exported from England to Mr. and Mrs. Robert M. Jackson of the Fourwinds Kennel.

4

The Modern Pekingese in Great Britain and Other Countries

by Andrew H. Brace

WHEN LOOKING at the history of the contemporary Pekingese in Great Britain, there can be only one starting point: Alderbourne. Mrs. Clarice Ashton Cross was a well-known society beauty of her day and was married to a famous and wealthy barrister. They had two sons and four daughters, each of whom was reputed to be very much under their mother's thumb, for it was claimed that Mrs. Ashton Cross was as imperious as she was beautiful.

In 1904, Mrs. Ashton Cross saw a strange-looking dog in Piccadilly, London. Intrigued by its oddness, she asked what it was and, on being informed as to the breed and its origins, resolved to have one. She bought a little bitch called Manchu Tzu from a Mrs. MacEwan, daughter of the artist Millais, and took it home to join her kennel of Bloodhounds and Arab horse stud.

Mrs. Ashton Cross soon decided that each of her daughters should have a Pekingese of her own and, armed with a decided air of professionalism and an inherent eye for quality, she began buying up the best available stock. A dog puppy born in 1904 was to become Ch. Chu-Erh of Alderbourne, the foundation of the Alderbourne Kennel and arguably the breed as we know it.

Immediately an Alderbourne Pekingese became something of a status symbol, and Pekingese that boasted but one of that kennel name (invariably bought in and frequently carrying no Alderbourne bloodlines whatsoever in their pedigrees) were immediately proudly dubbed "Alderbourne" by their boastful owners.

The Ashton Cross sisters ran a flourishing business with their dog shop in England's capital, and the Alderbourne Kennel became a vast establishment. All the fanciers who were to become attracted to the breed began with Alderbourne or Alderbourne-related stock, and many kennels that were to become household names of the future owed their success to linebreeding to dogs such as Chu-Erh.

AN OVERVIEW OF LEADING BRITISH KENNELS

By the late twenties several prominent kennels had been born, notably those of Mary de Pledge (Caversham), Mrs. Stains (Manstone), Miss Allen (Sherhill), Hindley Taylor (Kyratown) and Mrs. Williams (Toydom). These with Mrs. Chandler's Ifields, Miss Mayhew's Mingshangs and Mr. Higg's Yusens prospered before World Ward II, in turn laying the foundations for other kennels.

Mabel Cliff (later to become Mrs. Fryer), an established breeder of Chow Chows, acquired Puff Ball of Chungking from Elfreda Evans, the well-known Shih Tzu breeder, though Puff Ball had been bred at the Yusen Kennel. Puff Ball became a sire of great note though he himself never won his title.

Up until the fifties the breed fielded several indomitable kennels that boasted formidable owners. At the championship shows lesser mortals competed against the likes of the Ashton Cross sisters, Mary de Pledge and Hindley Taylor, yet several fiercely enthusiastic breeder/exhibitors managed to get past them on occasion. Indeed, in 1949 of all the new champions, only two were not owned by Alderbourne or Kyratown! One of these was the breathtakingly beautiful bitch Ch. Firefly of Calartha, a first champion for Sammy North who lived in the depths of Cornwall. Firefly was considered by many to be ahead of her time.

In the early fifties the Caversham brought out an exciting young dog that was to make the Pekingese world sit up and take note. Ch. Caversham Ku Ku of Yam was in many ways the turning point in contemporary Pekingese history and is still considered by many experts to be the model for the breed some thirty years later. Three breeders who were to become prominent in the Pekingese fancy made up their first champions in 1954 through using the great Ku Ku: Lilian Drake (Drakehurst), Yvonne Bentinck (Copplestone) and Ella Page, later to become Mrs. Francis Pilgrim (Chintoi).

Toward the end of the fifties new prefixes emerged with success. Among these were Wanstrow, Changte, Loofoo, Linsown, Kettlemere and Coughton.

In the early sixties the Pekingese world saw the appearance of one of its most colorful characters in Jean Eisenman. Using Caversham stock Mrs. Eisenman embarked on a daringly close program of line- and inbreeding to such an extent that she quickly established an instantly recognizable "type," the

Jamestowns being clear reds possessing shapely bodies and beautifully open faces with wondrous eyes. Many of today's currently active kennels used Jamestown stock as a base on which to build and have met with more than satisfying results.

In the sixties the Cherangani Kennel of Eileen Stewart rose to prominence, and while several champions carried the prefix, none will be better remembered than Ch. Cherangani Chips, a small dog that found favor with the true connoisseurs of the breed. Chips was to become quite an influential sire, too, siring among others Ailison Wilson's most famous champion, Who's Who of Wanstrow.

With the seventies emerged several breeders who made considerable impact on the show scene but have since become less active through retirement or advancing years.

As a very young lady Mary Hilton piloted her Wongville dogs through to top honors, and many started their own kennels with her breeding. One of these was Mrs. Phyl Finch whose Lisret Kennel produced high-quality dogs in a small frame. Her Ch. Lara of Lisret, daughter of Ch. Yu Yang of Jamestown, comes to mind as a prime example. One of the big winners of the seventies was Ch. Bellernes Dan Robino, owned and bred by Beryl Blackmore whose only champion he was. Sired by Dandino of Loofoo out of a daughter of Ch. Mr. Redcoat of Kanghe, he was a most impressive dog that amassed a number of CCs. He, like so many, inherited many good points from Redcoat, one of several dogs owned by Queenie Mould, one of the great characters of the Midlands fraternity.

It was a Redcoat son that became the first champion for Mr. and Mrs. Gordon Payne, Ch. Genderlee Sargent Pepper of Palaquin. He was bred by Geoffrey Davies, who for many years was associated with the Cherangani Kennel of Mrs. Stewart.

In the north, Eveline Ball (Kofu) and Eva Healey (Hilleva) enjoyed much success, particularly with homebred bitches, while the early seventies saw the birth of the Cynling Kennel of Cynthia Sterling, who amazed all by piloting her first bitch, Only a Wish of Lotusgrange of Cynling, through to her title and beyond—presented with flair that belied her time in the breed.

Doreen Holiday's Holdene prefix has been responsible for some excellent Pekingese, her lines being based very much on Changte breeding.

Longtime Midland supporters of the breed have been Olive and Arnold Clay. While they have owned champions, they will be best remembered for Oakmere Dolly Daydream of Upcot, the most enchanting parti-colored sleeve bitch the breed has seen. She was a great favorite and had an ardent fan club!

Also in the Midlands is Hylda Garwood, who came into Pekingese after being successful with Chow Chows. Among her best-known dogs were the tiny Ch. Hyldewood Shantung and his ice-white son, Ch. Pleiku Snow Shan of Hyldewood. Diana Holman's Etive Kennel for many years supported all the major shows with a large team and often won well with youngsters that were subsequently exported. Her Ch. Etive Master Chimes won his crown and later traveled overseas, a son of the Chips son Ch. Cherangani Chips Chime.

Ch. Micklee Rocfard, owned and bred by Mr. and Mrs. Jack Mitchell, was by Ch. Micklee Romeo out of a granddaughter of Ch. Micklee Tara.

Mr. and Mrs. Jack Mitchell's Ch. Micklee Roc's Ru Ago won his first Challenge Certificate as a puppy under R. William Taylor and became an all-breed Best in Show winner with Reserve Best in Show at Crufts to his credit. He was by Ch. Micklee Rocfard out of a granddaughter of Ch. Micklee Trawden Jin Twee.

One of Mr. and Mrs. Jack Mitchell's champion bitches, Micklee Roc's Royale, a daughter of Ch. Micklee Rocfard out of a daughter of Ch. Micklee Romeo and Ch. Micklee Tasca.

A vivacious and stunningly groomed lady appeared on the Pekingese scene in the form of Joy Montrose, who brought a sense of theater to the show ring. She showed stock bought from the Changte Kennel and soon began winning with her homebred stock under the Kybourne prefix.

One remarkable Pekingese of the seventies was Caroline Bryant's sleeve dog, Ch. Lionacre Small Yo Yo. Not only did he win his title, but he went through to take all-breed Best in Show at the Bournemouth Championship show of 1973.

Sadly, the majority of the above-named breeders are no longer with us, so it might be pertinent to look at those kennels that are presently enjoying the limelight and examine their history.

Jack and Joyce Mitchell (Micklee)

Three of the most successful Pekingese kennels today are based in the north of England. Jack and Joyce Mitchell who live in Yorkshire bred their first litter of Pekingese in 1947 and later resolved to build up a kennel based on Chintoi, Copplestone and Loofoo bloodlines. It was not until 1966 that they hit the big time when they appeared in the ring with a young dog, Simon of Belrosa, that was sired by an Alderbourne dog out of a Copplestone bitch. Simon acquired the Mitchells' now world-famous Micklee prefix and became their first champion.

Since that time the kennel has campaigned many champions, including the Crufts Reserve Best in Show winner Ch. Micklee Roc's Ru Ago that won twenty-six CCs and the Group winner Ch. Micklee Tarjeo that won twenty-two CCs. Other homebred Group-winning Micklee males were Ch. Micklee Risqui and Ch. Micklee Rocfard. They have also campaigned seven bitches to their titles to date, many of which have subsequently been bred. The Mitchells' exports have won championships in Europe, South Africa, the United States, Australia and on the home front, they have also qualified four puppies for the annual "Puppy of the Year" competition, a highly prestigious sponsored event.

Mr. and Mrs. Mitchell put their success down to close linebreeding with occasional outcrosses that they feel are most important.

Pauline Bull (Changte)

Pauline Bull registered her Changte prefix more than half a century ago and is still breeding and exhibiting. Indeed, her present winning dog is Changte-bred for an incredible twenty-two generations! Of her many champions, none will be better remembered than the exquisite little Ch. Chuffy's Charm of Changte that not only won seventeen CCs but was the top sire in the breed for 1973–74–75 and outright winner of the Pekingese Club's progeny cup. Mrs. Bull has stuck very much to her own bloodlines, seldom outcrossing, and has established an instantly identifiable line. There have been Changte champions in the United States, Canada, Singapore and Hong Kong.

Pauline Bull's exquisite Ch. Chuffy's Charm of Changte, a Crufts Best of Breed winner with seventeen CCs and two Toy Groups, which was Top Sire in the breed in Britain for 1973–74–75. Homebred for many generations, he was by Prince Chuffy of Changte ex Dawn Star of Changte.

Pauline Bull's Ch. Tsungli San Fou of Changte also won seventeen CCs. He was a Toy Group winner and a grandson of Ch. Crown Prince of Changte, Ch. Tudor Treasure of Changte and Ch. Micklee Simon of Belrosa.

Liz and Paul Stannard (Shiarita)

By comparison, Liz and Paul Stannard's Shiarita Kennel is a relative baby; yet, having registered their prefix in 1968, they have enjoyed meteoric success in the ensuing twenty years.

Their first champion was the homebred Ch. Beckee of Shiarita, predominantly Loofoo bred. Then they made up another bitch of excellent type, Ch. Swallowdale Ladybird of Dawoo. They befriended Jean Eisenman whose Jamestown dogs they had begun to use, and when Mrs. Eisenman's health began to fail, the Stannards kindly took over several of her dogs. They obviously shared her enthusiasm for keeping to a strict regime of inbreeding, and, it could be said, have taken over where she left off. Through very close linebreeding the Shiarita Kennel has produced a steady flow of champions, many of which became great winners. They have bred and campaigned four Group winners, the best known of which is the legendary Ch. Shiarita Cassidy. The winner of twenty-two CCs, many Groups and seven Best in Show awards at Club Specialty Championship events, he has made an enormous impact on the breed as a sire. He was Top Sire in the breed for 1979–80–81 and Top Sire of all Toy Breeds in 1987. He has ten British champions to his credit and many more overseas. Cassidy children can be spotted at a glance since he is prepotent in stamping his incredibly beautiful eyes, wide, shallow face and glamorous coat and fringes.

While Cassidy's place in the history books is assured, the story of his daughter Ch. Shiarita Diamond Lil is perhaps more remarkable. Lil was by Cassidy out of his own daughter, was a substantial bitch of superb type and was kept by her breeder as a brood bitch. On being a little dismayed at the quality of judging at one particular show, Liz Stannard remarked that she kept better brood bitches at home than some who were winning top awards. A fellow exhibitor then challenged her to put such a brood bitch in the ring. She went home that night, carefully evaluated the bitches in the maternity wing and decided that Diamond Lil, already a proven mother, would move into the show block. She worked on her coat until she was right, brought her out as a mature adult and won twenty CCs and two Toy Groups with her!

Shiarita exports have established winning records in the United States, Australia and Europe.

Dorothy Dearn (Dorodea)

The Midlands-based Dorodea Kennel of Dorothy Dearn began in the late forties with Alderbourne stock, which was later complemented with Caversham and Jamestown lines. The Dorodea Kennel has a reputation for producing top-class bitches, and all but two of its many champions have been of the fair sex.

There have been several outstandingly successful Dorodea winners in Europe. Like so many Pekingese breeders, Mrs. Dearn believes in sticking to a line with the occasional outcross but admits that it can be difficult to find a line that suits.

The intensely linebred Ch. Shiarita Cassidy was by Ch. Shiarita Lingsam out of Ch. Shiarita Hello Dolly. He won twenty-two CCs and a Toy Group, and was Top Sire in the breed in Britain for 1979–80–81–87. Owner-bred by Liz Stannard.

Ch. Shiarita Peter Pan won seventeen CCs and was an all-breed Best in Show winner. He was by Ch. Shiarita Cassidy out of Shiarita Cinderella; owner-bred by Liz Stannard.

Ch. Shiarita Diamond Lil, a daughter of Ch. Shiarita Cassidy and Shiarita Wendy, litter sister to Ch. Peter Pan and a Cassidy daughter. She did not commence her show career until she had been bred from, and then won twenty CCs and two Toy Groups for owner-breeder Liz Stannard.

Dorothy Dearn's Ch. Dorodea Dark Rhythm is an example of a black with the attractive silver trim.

Dorothy Dearn's Ch. Dorodea Merry Song was sired by the superbly bred Dorodea Ty Tiga out of Ch. Dorodea Favored Song. Mrs. Dearn's kennel is well known for champion bitches that breed on.

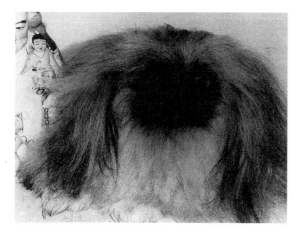

Tehila Brickwood's Ch. Teijon Ching Ching was her owner's first champion and amassed twenty-two CCs. She was by Ch. Samotha Gay Lad of Beaupres out of Beaupres Michelle of Teijon.

Tehila Brickwood (Teijon)

Slightly to the north of Dorodea is the Teijon Kennel of Tehila Brickwood, who has taken full advantage of Dorodea lines in her breeding program. Mrs. Brickwood started breeding in the fifties and enjoyed enormous success with her homebred Ch. Teijon Ching Ching in the late seventies. She finished up with twenty-two CCs, and since then she has taken two more homebred bitches through to their titles.

Mrs. Brickwood has overseas Teijon champions in Europe and the United States. She never keeps males and endeavors to linebreed with the occasional outcross before returning to the original lines. She believes that soundness and type are most important and will breed only from show-quality bitches.

May Robertshaw (Lotusgrange)

May Robertshaw, originally from the north of England but now based in the midwest, is another who chose Caversham and then Jamestown lines to establish her kennel. Formerly involved with Bulldogs, she registered her Lotusgrange prefix in 1954 and has since produced several homebred champions, having used only three outside dogs in the past twenty years, and then from parallel lines to the home kennel. Very much keeping to type, the Lotusgrange dogs are easily recognized, and Mrs. Robertshaw has sent dogs to Europe and the United States, where they have become champions.

Ch. Some Man of Lotusgrange returned to the home kennel in 1980 as the baby son of the heavily linebred Lotusgrange Jamesman and an Alderbourne-bred bitch. He became the top-winning Lotusgrange champion to date and established himself as a sire of note. Used on a Micklee/Pekehuis-bred bitch, he produced Ch. Pemyn Some Guy, which was owned by Joan Cross in partnership with Winifred Mee who for many years worked for Ethel Partridge and handled her Pekehuis dogs in the ring. Of these the best remembered will be multiple CC-winning Ch. St. Aubrey Pekehuis Petula with that unforgettable velvety black face. A direct descendant of Petula's daughter, Ch. Pekehuis Petal, was mated to Some Guy and produced Ch. Pekehuis Sir Guy, which has won many CCs for Miss Mee and is also a Group and Best in Show winner.

Elizabeth and Fiona Mirylees (Beaupres)

Quite close to the present home of the Lotusgrange Kennel is the Beaupres establishment founded by the late Elizabeth Mirylees and now continued by her daughter Fiona. At one time a very prolific kennel, the best known of the Beaupres Pekingese was probably the fabulously coated Ch. Beaupres Belle, which returned to the show ring to win her title at an incredible seven years of age. Many Beaupres exports became champions in all parts of the world, and though the kennel does not exhibit now as frequently as in the past, Miss Mirylees still judges the breed and is well known for her extremely eloquent critiques.

86

Tehila Brickwood's Ch. Teijon Linnetta, a homebred daughter of the successful sire Sungarth Kanga of Toydom and Teijon Ling Ty.

May Robertshaw's Ch. Some Man of Lotusgrange was sired by Lotusgrange Jamesman, while his dam, Arrow Blue Bonnet, was bred from two of the last Alderbourne Pekingese.

May Robertshaw's homebred Ch. Lotusgrange Again the Same, sired by Ch. Some Man of Lotusgrange out of a daughter of Ch. Lotusgrange Shorona.

Three champion bitches at one time owned by Ethel Partridge of the famous Pekehuis Kennel: Ch. St. Aubrey Pekehuis Honey Dew (top), Ch. Pekehuis Chero Queen (left), and Ch. St. Aubrey Pekehuis Petula (right), which was the winner of thirty-five CCs.

Winifred Mee has campaigned Ch. Pekehuis Sir Guy through to win many CCs, Toy Groups and a Best in Show at all-breed level. He is by Ch. Pemyn Some Guy out of Pekehuis Prima Donna.

The sensational Ch. Beaupres Belle, owned by Elizabeth Mirylees and her daughter Fiona, won her title at seven years of age. Bred by Mr. and Mrs. Alan Charlton, she was by Ch. Mr. Redcoat of Kanghe out of Ch. Kai Lyn of Brentoy. She was a sister to Betty Shoemaker's miniatures, Copplestone Miss Pinkcoat and Mr. Pinkcoat.

Antonia Horn (Belknap)

The southwest of England has always been a strong area for Pekingese, and no kennel in the area has proved more successful than that of Antonia Horn, whose Belknap Pekingese are synonymous with small, high-quality dogs and typey dual-purpose show/brood bitches. Founded in 1963, Mrs. Horn blended Caversham, Coughton and Jamestown lines with much success, having read, studied and visited strongholds of the breed. Mrs. Horn has never campaigned champions to multiple CCs; keeping a fairly large kennel, she invariably had a young star waiting in the wings and ready to take over from her reigning champion. Her first champion was Ch. Suzie Wong of Jamestown, so typical of her breeding, and her biggest winner, Ch. Belknap Pocket Peke, won ten CCs.

Mrs. Horn has made up twelve British champions, and more carry her prefix. Ch. Belknap El Dorado was an all-breed Best in Show winner at championship level, while Ch. Belknap Bravo and Ch. Belknap Pocket Peke were Group winners. The Belknaps are not kenneled because their happiness and comfort are of prime importance to their owner. Several Pekingese exported by Mrs. Horn have achieved great notoriety in their adopted homelands, notably Am. Ch. Velvetina and N.Z. Ch. Brave Star by Belknap.

Mrs. Horn puts her sustained success down to consistent linebreeding, often mating half brother to half sister, with occasional outcrossing via the bitches. She has always tried to breed small males and larger, robust bitches, and is quoted as saying, "It is the cock that crows, but the hen that lays the eggs!"

A Belknap stud dog, Ch. Belknap Bravo, was responsible for May Young's producing a champion brother and sister, Adlungs Rah Rah and Adlungs Sweet Charity. Again domiciled in the southwest, Miss Young began breeding dogs in 1944 and became a force to be reckoned with in both Chow Chows and Rough Collies. Subsequently her attentions focused on the Pekingese, and she bought the CC-winning bitch Singlewell Little Else from Pamela Edmond and took her through to her title.

Eileen Newman (Rosayleen)

The Rosayleen Pekingese of Eileen Newman began in 1973 though she had owned Pekes as pets for some years previously. Miss Young originally handled for Mrs. Newman, but recently she has taken to the ring herself. There have now been several Rosayleen champions, the best known of which is Ch. Rosayleen the Gaffer of Sunsalve, jointly owned with Terry Nethercott. He won seventeen CCs and three Toy Groups, and his breeder, Mrs. Newman, attributes success to close linebreeding and "a lot of damned hard work!" She has exported to Canada, the United States, South Africa and many European countries where her exports have more than held their own.

Ch. Suzie Wong of Jamestown, bred by Jean Eisenman, was the foundation bitch of Antonia Horn's Belknap Kennel.

Antonia Horn's Ch. Belknap Sugar Plum was a grandson of Ch. Ping Yang of Coughton and Belknap Jin Song of Jamestown.

Antonia Horn's Ch. Belknap El Dorado, a grandson of Ch. Yu Yang of Jamestown and Belknap Jin Song of Jamestown, lies behind the dam of the 1990 Westminster Best in Show winner, Edward B. Jenner's Ch. Wendessa Crown Prince.

Black-and-tans have always been a favorite of Antonia Horn. Here is the outstanding Ch. Scarteena by Belknap, a daughter of Ch. Belknap Nero out of a daughter of Ch. Belknap Pocket Peke.

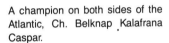
A champion on both sides of the Atlantic, Ch. Belknap Kalafrana Caspar.

Ch. Singlewell Little Else won her first CC under Nigel Aubrey-Jones. A daughter of Ch. Singlewell Wee Sedso and Singlewell Donna Tanzee, she was sold by her breeder, Pamela Edmond, to May Young, for whose Adlung Kennel she became the first Pekingese champion.

91

May Young's Ch. Adlung's Rah Rah, a son of Ch. Belknap Bravo out of a daughter of Ch. Singlewell Wee Sedso.

May Young's Ch. Adlung's Sweet Charity was litter sister to Ch. Adlung's Rah Rah. Both won their first Challenge Certificates at the same show.

Nigel Aubrey-Jones's Best in Show winner at the Pekingese Club was Jennifer Sims's Genisim a Different Drummer.

Pamela Edmond (Singlewell)

In the south of England will be found Pamela Edmond's famous Singlewell Kennel, the prefix being registered in 1947. Starting with two bitches by a Caversham dog, Mrs. Edmond and her mother used Alderbourne stud dogs to establish their original foundation.

Mrs. Edmond firmly believes that the strength of her kennel has been its bitches. Like so many Pekingese breeders she is a firm advocate of linebreeding, favoring half brother to half sister, uncle to niece or aunt to nephew, with the occasional strong outcross. This formula has produced a string of champions both in the United Kingdom and overseas. Her first champion, Singlewell Sun Chu, was out of a superb little bitch that came from a half brother to half sister mating on Tul Tuo of Alderbourne. Of the many Singlewell champions, four won Groups, and the most celebrated of these was the majestic bitch Ch. Singlewell T'Sai Magic which won fifteen CCs. Her career was all the more remarkable, however, because, apart from her showing successes, she produced in four litters (no Caesarean sections!) five British champions, one German champion, one French champion, one American champion and one Swedish champion.

Ch. Singlewell Wee Sedso was never widely used at stud, but through his son, Sungarth Kanga of Toydom, his name will live on in many pedigrees for years to come.

Beryl Prior (Sungarth)

Sungarth Kanga of Toydom was one of many significant Pekingese bred by the late Beryl Prior in a relatively short career in the breed. Hitherto Mrs. Prior had taken her Sungarth Kennel to the top in Bulldogs and Basset Hounds—two very difficult breeds—when she started up in Pekingese with Carole of Carona. Carole produced the lovely Ch. Sungarth Camellia when mated to the strongly linebred Ch. Chyanchy Ah Yang of Jamestown, and Mrs. Prior then produced Ch. Sungarth Hi Jinks of Sunsalve, which put Mr. Nethercott's Sunsalve Kennel on the map, and Sungarth Kanga of Toydom.

Vandellia Williams and Adele Summers (Toydom)

The Toydom prefix was originally registered by the late Alexandria Williams in the early 1920s, but gradually the kennel disappeared. In the early 1970s, however, Mrs. Williams's daughter, Vandella, now in partnership with Adele Summers, resolved to resurrect the kennel and began searching for foundation stock through which to pick up the old Toydom bloodlines. Thus Sungarth Kanga of Toydom was located, and he became the cornerstone of the kennel that later incorporated Jamestown and Micklee lines.

The partnership has been highly successful in the United Kingdom and has exported winners on a large scale. Indeed, Toydom exports are responsible in the main for the great success of the Scandinavian Hotpoint Pekingese of Borghild Sorensen.

Pamela Edmond's Ch. Singlewell Wee Sedso was a prominent stud dog. He was sired by Honorable Mr. Twee of Kanghe out of a daughter of Ch. Singlewell Sun Chu, the kennel's first champion.

Pamela Edmond's magnificent bitch, Ch. Singlewell T'Sai Magic, was not only a multiple CC and Toy Group winner but became the dam of many champions, all whelped naturally. Bred to Ch. Micklee Roc's Ru Ago she produced Ch. Singlewell Magic Ruler, which is now proving a stud force to be reckoned with.

Terry Nethercott's Ch. Sungarth Hi Jinks of Sunsalve, a double grandson of Chu Yu Yang of Jamestown, was the first champion for the Sunsalve Kennel in the 1970s.

Adele Summers and Vandella Williams's Toydom Trump Card, a son of Sungarth Kanga of Toydom, was a significant sire, numbering among his immediate progeny the highly successful sire Ch. Jay Trump of Sunsalve.

Ch. Toydom Modesty Forbids, owned and bred by Adele Summers and Vandella Williams, sired Ch. Belknap Bravo, Ch. Belknap Blush, Ch. Toydom Modesty Permits and several overseas champions. He was by Ch. Belknap El Dorado out of a daughter of Sungarth Kanga of Toydom.

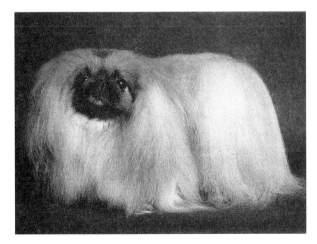

Terry Nethercott's Ch. Sunsalve My Love, one of many champions sired by Ch. Jay Trump of Sunsalve. Her dam was sister to the lovely Ch. Sungarth Camellia.

There have been many Toydom champions in the United Kingdom, including the Group-winning Ch. Toydom Modesty Forbids and the Crufts Best of Breed winner Ch. Toydom A Touch of Class.

Vandella Williams and Adele Summers attribute their success to "pure luck and instinct," a rather modest assessment. They also firmly believe in breeding only from show-quality bitches.

Terry Nethercott and Eddie Hurdle (Sunsalve)

The Sunsalve prefix is now owned by Terry Nethercott and his partner, Eddie Hurdle. It was registered in 1969 and is founded on Caversham and Jamestown lines, recently working closely with the Toydom Kennel's bloodlines. Several champions have been bred, and both Ch. Jay Trump of Sunsalve and Ch. Rosayleen the Gaffer of Sunsalve are Group winners. Jay Trump, however, has proved a remarkable stud force with some twelve British and thirty-one overseas champions to his credit. He was Top Sire in the breed for 1982–83–84–85–86. There have been several overseas champions carrying the Sunsalve prefix, and Mr. Nethercott believes in half brother to half sister matings, also grandsire to granddaughter, with a complete outcross in the fourth generation.

Barbara Lashmar (Ralshams)

In the mid-fifties the Ralshams prefix was registered by Barbara Lashmar and is now owned jointly with her daughter Carole. Originally a devotee of white Poodles, Mrs. Lashmar was quickly bewitched by the charms of the Pekingese, and using Caversham and Alderbourne lines, then outcrossing to Tzumiao and Cherangani, she soon established a strong kennel that has been particularly known for outstanding bitches. The kennel's first champion, the lovely Ch. Ralshams Ku Donna, is the ancestor of all subsequent champions including the 1988 Crufts Bitch CC winner, Ch. Ralshams Lady Ku Donna. The exquisite Ch. Ralshams Lovely Lady won her title in the United Kingdom and then made a name for herself in the United States. There have been many other champions in Australia and the Americas.

Mrs. Lashmar believes in close linebreeding with the occasional outcross, always aiming for soundness, quality and showmanship.

Lilian Snook (Laparata)

Another successful southeastern breeder who has succeeded in establishing a kennel known for intense quality is Lilian Snook of the Laparata Pekingese. Founded in 1966 on descendants of the great Ch. Caversham Ku Ku of Yam, Mrs. Snook has produced several champions with the wide shallow face and glamorous coats for which the prefix is known. Again, linebreeding is the secret,

Barbara Lashmar's Ch. Ralshams Ku Donna, the first in a long line of Ralshams champions.

Lilian Snook's handsome Ch. Laparata Celestial Star was sired by Ch. Etive Copplestone Pu Zin Julier out of Laparata Celeste, a daughter of Ch. Cherangani Chips and Laparata Ralshams Claudia.

Lilian Snook's Ch. Laparata Precious Madame, one of the kennel's linebred champion bitches.

and when an occasional outcross is called for, Mrs. Snook prefers to use a dog that is not itself closely bred because she feels this maintains the dominance of her own breeding. Mrs. Snook does not campaign champions; they are retired once titled. Her most famous export is without doubt the great Ch. St. Aubrey Laparata Dragon that founded a veritable dynasty in his new homeland.

IRISH AND SCOTTISH BREEDERS OF NOTE

Having looked at the successful kennels of England, one should not ignore Ireland and Scotland because they too have more than played their part. In Ireland, Winifred Crowe's Colindenes have for many years put into the ring top-class Pekingese that frequently win in England, and she has taken several through to their titles. Recently Mrs. Mellor's Clareviews and Mrs. Watters's Yankuis have also held their own.

In Scotland the Craigfoss Kennel of Sloane Stanley and Miss Piggott has produced many outstanding Pekingese including the mouth-watering Ch. St. Aubrey Fairy Ku of Craigfoss. George Quinn's Tuadore Kennel will long be remembered for its campaigning of the lavishly coated Ch. Tuadore Master Bertie, once reputed to be the oldest living champion of any breed in Britain.

Albert Easdon and Philip Martin (Yakee)

Recently a much younger Scottish-based kennel has taken the breed by storm, namely the Yakee Kennel of Albert Easdon and Philip Martin. Previously the partners had produced champions in Boston Terriers and Shih Tzus (among them the top-winning Shih Tzu of all time in the United Kingdom), but when they mated a Singlewell-sired bitch from the Scottish lines of Niloc and Atter-cliffe to a Toydom dog, they bred their first champion Pekingese, Yakee Patent Pending.

They then took a Toydom-sired bitch to Ch. Shiarita Cassidy and produced a spectacularly glamorous brother and sister that won their titles at a very young age, Ch. Yakee Gentleman Prefer and her brother Ch. Yakee For Your Eyes Only, which covered himself in glory by winning Best in Show at the huge Birmingham National Championship show of 1988 and later Reserve Best in Show at Crufts in 1989.

Like so many, the partners believe in linebreeding but also use the best stud dogs available, no matter what obstacles. And living in Scotland, campaigning their team is possibly more exhausting than for many other exhibitors.

THE BEST OF SOUTH WALES

South Wales has always had a strong Pekingese fancy. Indeed, one of the breed's great authorities, Nigel Aubrey-Jones, is one of its most famous sons. Originally the St. Aubrey Kennel was based in the principality, as was the

Ch. St. Aubrey Fairy Ku of Craigfoss, bred by Sloane Stanley and Miss Piggott, won seventeen CCs in a very short show career when in the ownership of Nigel Aubrey-Jones and R. William Taylor.

Ch. Yakee Patent Pending was the first champion for the now highly successful Yakee Kennel of Albert Easdon and Philip Martin, who had previously made their mark in Boston Terriers and Shih Tzus.

Ch. Yakee Gentlemen Prefer, one of two champion littermates by Ch. Shiarita Cassidy, bred and owned by Albert Easdon and Philip Martin. This glamorous bitch died at a very early age.

Albert Easdon and Philip Martin's Ch. Yakee For Your Eyes Only, a multiple CC winner with all-breed Best in Show and Reserve Best in Show at Crufts to his credit. He was litter brother to Ch. Yakee Gentlemen Prefer.

Chyanchy Kennel of Lily Sawyer. Longtime breeder Nancy Kerkin has also met with a degree of success with her Wei Sing Prai Kennel. Her Ch. Pixie of Wei Sing Prai was a well-known winner that then produced an even lovelier daughter, Ch. Wei Sing Prai Pollyanna, which won many CCs and the Pekingese Club's Gold Medal.

Founding her kennel in 1956 on Caversham and Jamestown lines, Mrs. Kerkin has never exhibited as much as she would have liked due to ill health, and her breeding program has been rather limited.

Other champions that have come from South Wales include the sensational little dog Ch. Bumper Beaujolais of Bilsby, so ably prepared and handled by his young owner, Gary Carter. He in turn sired the equally striking and equally small Ch. Bilsby Court Jester of Priorsway.

While never a very active exhibitor, mention must be made of Doris Pritchard, whose Mellifont Kennel has not only produced several CC winners for other exhibitors but has also produced the foundation stock on which others have built. Her kennel is based on old Changte lines coupled with Bonaventure and Wongville.

Gary Thomas (Jonsville)

One young and enthusiastic exhibitor who is currently making a name for himself is Gary Thomas, who, with his parents, owns the Jonsville Kennel. Beginning with Mellifont stock he bred his first champion, Ch. Jonsville Magic Touch, by mating a Mellifont bitch to a Sungarth-sired dog owned by Philip and Jackie Jones, who own the Bramblefields Kennel and who recently made up their first two homebred champions. A homebred Jonsville bitch was then taken to the predominantly Loofoo-bred Ch. Hidden Talent of Toydom to produce Ch. Jonsville Daytime Lover, which became the first Pekingese in over forty years to win three Bests in Show at general championship shows in the United Kingdom in one year. In 1990 he was sold to Germany.

Perhaps the most refreshing aspect of the contemporary scene is that there are several talented and enthusiastic young breeder/exhibitors whose quality dogs are meeting with the success they deserve, refuting the theory that the plum awards are always reserved for the long-serving establishment. Given that their enthusiasm continues, the breed would appear to be in good hands.

The Pekingese obviously has a following in every country of the world where purebred dogs are shown; however, some nations have made greater advances than others in the production of high-quality Pekingese.

AUSTRALIA

In Australia several kennels have bred consistently good Pekingese to such an extent that they have exported stock to the United States and Canada that has proved valuable in breeding programs. The fact that many Australians tend to

Nancy Kerkin's first champion was Pixie of Wei-Sing-Prai, a daughter of Ch. Chyanchy Ah Yang of Jamestown out of a daughter of Rookie of Calartha. She is to be found behind the breeding of the 1990 Westminster Best in Show winner.

Ch. Wei-Sing-Prai Pollyanna, bred and owned by Nancy Kerkin, was out of Ch. Pixie of Wei-Sing-Prai and sired by the big-winning Ch. Bellernes Dan Robino.

102

The youngest exhibitor to have achieved top honors with a Pekingese in Britain must be Gary Thomas, seen here winning Best in Show at the South Wales Kennel Association Championship show in 1988. During that year Ch. Jonsville Daytime Lover won three all-breed Best in Show awards (the first Pekingese to do so in forty years) and Top Toy Dog of all breeds.

Am. & Can. Ch. Lingling Gypsy Sue was imported by R. William Taylor from Australia, where she was a winner at the Melbourne Royal show. She subsequently produced Ch. St. Aubrey Romany of Elsdon, top-winning Pekingese in Canada for one year.

prefer a taller, more necky and extremely overcoated dog than the average British or American fancier has meant that it has been easier to secure dogs of acceptable type because these invariably were not the big winners Down Under. New Zealand, too, has produced some top-class dogs that have found their way to other parts of the world.

SOUTH AFRICA

In South Africa the Pekingese scene has for years been a lively one with lots of British imports of the four- and two-legged variety. In recent years Jennifer Sims and Mr. and Mrs. Alan Charlton have returned to their native United Kingdom where they have continued their breeding with much success.

SCANDINAVIA

Scandinavia, in dog terms, is one of the most advanced countries today, producing many outstanding dogs and outstanding all-breed judges. Norway in particular has made great strides with Pekingese.

5

The Pekingese Standard

with discussion by R. William Taylor

THE KENNEL CLUB (BRITAIN) BREED STANDARD

General Appearance: Small, well-balanced, thickset dog of dignity and quality.

Characteristics: Leonine in appearance with alert and intelligent expression.

Temperament: Fearless, loyal, aloof but not timid or aggressive.

Head and Skull: Head large; proportionately wider than deep. Skull broad, wide and flat between ears, not domed; wide between eyes. Nose short and broad; nostrils large, open and black; muzzle wide, well wrinkled, with firm underjaw. Profile flat with nose well set between eyes. Pronounced stop. Black pigment essential on nose, lips and eye rims.

Eyes: Large, clear, round, dark and lustrous.

Ears: Heart-shaped, set level with the skull and carried close to the head, with long profuse feathering. Leather not to come below line of muzzle.

Mouth: Level lips; must not show teeth or tongue. Firm underjaw essential.

Neck: Very short and thick.

Forequarters: Short, thick, heavily boned forelegs; bones of forelegs slightly bowed, firm at shoulder. Soundness essential.

Body: Short, broad chest and good spring of ribs; well slung between forelegs with distinct waist; level back.

Hindquarters: Hind legs lighter than forelegs but firm and well shaped. Close behind but not cow hocked. Soundness essential.

Feet: Large and flat, not round. Standing well up on feet, not on pasterns. Front feet turned slightly out.

Tail: Set high, carried tightly, slightly curved over back to either side. Long feathering.

Gait/Movement: Slow, dignified, rolling gait in front. Typical movement not to be confused with a roll caused by slackness of shoulders. Close action behind. Absolute soundness essential.

Coat: Long, straight, with profuse mane extending beyond shoulders and forming a cape around neck; top coat coarse with thick undercoat. Profuse feathering on ears, back of legs, tail and toes.

Color: All colors and markings are permissible and of equal merit, except albino or liver. Parti-colors evenly broken.

Size: Ideal weight not exceeding 11 pounds (5 kilograms) for dogs and 12 pounds (5 ½ kilograms) for bitches. Dogs should look small but be surprisingly heavy when picked up; heavy bone and a sturdy well-built body are essentials of the breed.

Faults: Any departure from the foregoing points should be considered a fault, and the seriousness with which the fault is regarded should be in exact proportion to its degree.

Note: Male animals should have two apparently normal testicles fully descended into the scrotum.

October 1989

THE AMERICAN KENNEL CLUB PEKINGESE STANDARD

Expression: Must suggest the Chinese origin of the Pekingese in its quaintness and individuality, resemblance to the lion in directness and independence, and should imply courage, boldness, self-esteem and combativeness rather than prettiness, daintiness or delicacy.

Skull: Massive, broad, wide and flat between the ears (not dome-shaped); wide between the eyes.

Nose: Black, broad, very short and flat.

Eyes: Large, dark, prominent, round, lustrous.

Stop: Deep.

Ears: Heart-shaped, not set too high; leather never long enough to come below the muzzle, nor carried erect, but rather drooping; long feather.

Muzzle: Wrinkled, very short and broad, not overshot or pointed. Strong, broad underjaw; teeth must not show.

Shape of Body: Heavy in front, well-sprung ribs, broad chest, falling away lighter behind, lionlike, back level. Not too long in body; allowance made for longer body in bitch.

Legs: Short forelegs; bones of forearm bowed, firm at shoulder; hind legs lighter but firm and well shaped.

Feet: Flat, toes turned out, not round; should stand well up on feet, not ankles.

Action: Fearless, free and strong, with slight roll.

Coat, Feather and Condition: Long with thick undercoat, straight and flat, not curly, not wavy, rather coarse but soft; feather on thighs, legs and toes, long and profuse.

Mane: Profuse, extending beyond the shoulder blades, forming ruff or frill around the neck.

Color: All colors are allowable; red, fawn, black, black and tan, sable, brindle, white and parti-color well defined; black masks and spectacles around the eyes, with lines to ear, are desirable.

Definition of a parti-colored Pekingese: The coloring of a parti-color must be broken on the body. No large portion of any one color should exist. White should be shown on the saddle. A dog of any solid color with white feet and chest is *not* a parti-color.

Tail: Set high, lying well over back to either side; long, profuse, straight feather.

Size: Being a Toy Dog, medium size preferred, providing type and points are not sacrificed; extreme limit 14 pounds.

Penalization: Protruding tongue; badly blemished eyes; overshot and wry mouth.

Disqualification: Dudley nose; weight over 14 pounds.

Expression	5	Shape of Body	15
Skull	10	Legs and Feet	15
Nose	5	Coat, Feather and Condition	15
Eyes	5	Tail	5
Stop	5	Action	10
Ears	5		
Muzzle	5		
		Total	100

April 1956

R. WILLIAM TAYLOR DISCUSSES REVISING THE PEKINGESE STANDARD—OCTOBER 10, 1983

For many years the Pekingese breed had two breed Standards, one by the Pekingese Club and another by the Pekin Palace Dog Association whose seventy-fifth anniversary was celebrated in 1983. In 1908 both breed Standards were under the title "Description and Standard of Points," with each club having a scale of points for certain features of the breed that they felt was their degree of importance.

The allotting of points to various parts of the Standard has been eliminated for some time now. Perhaps the Kennel Club thought too much attention would be given to one or two points at the expense of others, a not altogether unreasonable assumption.

Head Breed

The Pekingese has constantly been referred to as a "head" breed, which is not surprising considering that the Pekingese Club's 1908 Standard of points for head alone amounted to thirty-five, ten more than the Standard of the PPDA. Both Standards gave equal points to action—ten. The Pekingese Club stressed tail at ten points, the PPDA giving only five points. The PPDA considered that shape of body merited twenty points, the Pekingese Club only ten. Legs and feet also appeared to be of more concern to the PPDA, the points given in their Standard totaling fifteen to the Pekingese Club's ten. Size and color merited no points in the PPDA Standard compared to five points each by the Pekingese Club. This is somewhat surprising because it was on the size question that the founding members of the Pekin Palace broke with the Pekingese Club.

Coat, feather and mane in both Standards totaled fifteen. A keen mathematician will note from the above figures that the Pekingese Club Standard totals one hundred while the PPDA totals only ninety. This is because a heading of "General Appearance" in the Standard of the PPDA was not included in the Pekingese Club Standard, and it was allotted ten points. Under general appearance the 1908 PPDA Standard read: "A sturdy, compact little dog of dignified and fearless carriage and sound and healthy condition," an apt description of the Pekingese dog even to this day. When the Kennel Club decreed that there be only one Standard, this section was incorporated into the official Standard and has headed the Standard ever since. The present description under general appearance reads: "Should be a small, well-balanced, thickset dog of great dignity and quality. He should carry himself fearlessly in the ring with an alert, intelligent expression." This is a satisfying description of the Pekingese, saying in two sentences what the individual points of the Standard cannot convey. Its description is of the dog as a whole, stressing balance and incorporating the word "quality," two words that are missing in the Standard of many breeds.

Taken for Granted?

With the change in format of breed Standards about to take place, the committees of the various Pekingese clubs have been sent a revised Pekingese Standard for their comments. While some may argue that any change is not necessary, if changes are to be made they should be for the better, with a concise Standard of the breed. In the case of the revised Pekingese Standard now under consideration, it can only be described as woefully lacking in correcting past omissions, and in the case of the section under "Mouth," a total lack of comprehension of the point in question.

What is curious about the suggested revision is that while the present Standard distinctly states "absolute soundness essential" not once but three times, the revised Pekingese Standard makes no mention of soundness whatever. Perhaps the Kennel Club believes we should take that for granted, but in a breed where the very make and shape makes it a difficult yet challenging task to produce a perfectly sound dog, it is surprising that the word "soundness" is omitted. Even the PPDA included the word in its Standard of 1908. The lack of the word "soundness" in the revised Pekingese Standard might appear to give comfort to those whose dogs are not 100 percent fit and sound. I can imagine the retort of a great many to any suggestion of unsoundness, that "it is not mentioned in the Standard." This could very well be corrected by including soundness under the heading "General Gait."

Unique Feature

One of the last changes to the Standard that was actually an addition was made in the 1970s when gait was described. It had been in the original Pekingese Club and PPDA Standards, although not too clearly defined, but it appeared to be dropped when the Standard was overhauled in the late 1940s. The addition was overdue because the gait is a unique feature of the breed. The revised Pekingese Standard, which I will refer to as RPS, appears to water down the present description, removing any mention of hind action.

The RPS reads, "Gait: slow, dignified, rolling gait. Typical movement not to be confused with a roll caused by slackness of shoulders." While trying to explain the rolling gait of the forequarters, it completely ignores the hind action that does not roll. To describe the action of a Pekingese I believe the reasons should be given just why the Pekingese has such a distinctive movement. Its shape of body, together with bowed front legs and narrow quarters, are just those reasons. A better description of gait would read: "Fore-action: slow, dignified, rolling gait caused by body being heavy in front and lighter in quarters, with forelegs being bowed and hindquarters being close and parallel. The typical rolling action is not to be confused with a roll caused by slackness of shoulders that will not flow freely. Hind action: close, steady and free. Soundness essential."

Dissimilar

Under the description "Feet," the present Standard and the RPS refer only to the front feet; no mention at all is made of the hind feet, which are dissimilar to those of the front. The RPS reads: "Large and flat, not round. Standing well up on feet, not on pasterns. Front feet turned slightly out.'' The addition of "Hind feet: smaller, turning neither in nor out but forward" would clarify the matter. The description of "Body" in the RPS reads: "Short, broad chest and good spring of ribs, falling away lighter behind with distinct waist, level back, well slung between legs. Leonine." The description "well slung between legs" is ambiguous, for while the chest is slung between the forelegs, the rear is certainly not slung between the hind legs. A better description would read: "Short, broad chest with good spring of rib well slung between forelegs, tapering to lighter loins with distinct waist, level back. Lionlike." The description "tapering to lighter loins" is far more descriptive than "falling away lighter behind," and the word "lionlike" has been an accepted description of the breed for many years. To replace it with "leonine," which in the dictionary reads "lionlike," seems to me unnecessary.

Notable Exception

Under "Hindquarters" the RPS reads: "Hind legs lighter than forelegs but firm and well shaped. Close behind but not cow hocked." The words "well shaped" mean nothing or could mean anything. Better still would be a description reading: "Hindquarters: Hind legs lighter in bone than forelegs; well angulated and defined hock. When viewed from behind should be close and parallel to one another. Never cow hocked or bandy legged." The description "close behind" in the RPS is far too vague, and if cow hocks are to be specifically mentioned, then their opposite or bandy legs, which is an equally bad fault, should be mentioned as well.

The description of the tail in the RPS, which is the same as the present Standard, has never to my mind been a true picture of the correct Pekingese tail carriage. It reads: "Tail: Set high, carried tightly, slightly curved over back to either side. Long feathering." True, the tail should be set high and have long feathering, but I can never reconcile that a tail carried slightly curved over the back to either side could also be carried tightly. In the dictionary one description of tight is taut, which is a contradiction of slightly curved. A tight tail carriage refers to one that would be held more tightly to the back than the true Pekingese tail carriage, which should be loose yet still set high and carried well over the back. It is flowing that the description "tight" does not convey. A better description would be "Tail: Set high, carried in a slight curve well over the back to either side. Long feathering."

A Frame

Under "Head and Skull" the RPS reads: "Head large, skull broad, wide and flat between the ears, not domed, wide between eyes. Nose short and broad, nostrils large, open and black, muzzle wide, well wrinkled, with firm underjaw. Profile flat with nose well set between eyes. Pronounced stop." This is basically the same as the present Standard with one notable exception: the word "large" replaces "massive." Also, the word "pronounced" replaces "deep" in describing the stop. The word "massive" in the present Standard conveys the impression that the head of the Pekingese is large in comparison to the body, which is exactly as it should be and therefore in my opinion should be retained. And "deep" is a better description of the Pekingese stop than the newfound "pronounced."

In my copy of the Revised Pekingese Standard, the description under "Eyes" uses four words: large, clear, dark and lustrous. I can only assume that an error in omitting shape has been made because this was described as round in the present Standard and definitely should be retained. In the subheading "General Appearance" in the RPS the description of expression is left out. It could therefore be added to the proposed Standard, which could read: "Eyes: Large, round, clear, dark and lustrous. Alert, intelligent expression."

Under "Ears" the description of the RPS reads: "Heart-shaped, set level with the skull and carried close to the head, with long profuse feathering. Leather not to come below line of muzzle." The addition of "framing the face" after profuse feathering might give a clearer picture of the proper ear set.

Lionlike

The Kennel Club has asked for particular thought to be given to the headings "Characteristics" and "Temperament" in the RPS. Temperament can be easily dealt with by the inclusion of the words "bold," "fearless" and "independent." The word "characteristics," according to my dictionary, means "that which marks or constitutes the character." "Character" means distinctive mark, any essential feature or peculiarity. John A. Vlasto, in his excellent book *The Popular Pekingese,* wrote: "Character is a term that covers the distinctive points of any breed. Thus we can say from one hundred yards away, 'That is a Pekingese.' Both type and balance have a share in giving the character, but in our breed it resides chiefly in the body, the forelegs and the gait." It would therefore seem to me that any description under the heading "Characteristics" could very well be handled and taken care of under the heading "General Appearance." Both appear to be discussing much the same thing. A suggestion for the wording under "General Appearance" would read: "Small, well-balanced, thickset dog with heavy front and lighter quarters. Of great quality and dignity. Carries himself fearlessly with distinctive rolling gait. Lionlike."

As to the description of mouth in the RPS, I can only describe it as a disaster. It reads: "Mouth: Level lips, not showing teeth or tongue. Reverse scissor bite." Underjaw is already mentioned under "Head and Skull" but could also be included in this section where it properly belongs. I would recommend the following description of mouth in any revised Standard. "Mouth: Level lips, not showing teeth or tongue; broad, level underjaw. Undershot." The term "reverse scissor bite" is the contentious description in the RPS and to my mind totally unacceptable. A reverse scissor bite is when the bottom teeth are just in front of the upper and tightly touching one another when the mouth is closed. One can only describe this as a weak chin. I would venture to say that the great majority of champions in the past were at least one-eighth of an inch undershot and some a great deal more. One need only to look at the pictures of some of the big winners, dogs such as the great Ch. Ku Chik Ku of Loofoo that won three consecutive CCs at Crufts, to see that he had a strong underjaw, nothing even remotely suggesting a reverse scissor bite.

If the breed is suffering from a surfeit of weak chins, then this is certainly not the time to condone or encourage them. This is perhaps a plain case of changing the Standard to suit a current trend that is prevalent in the breed. A breed Standard should cite the ideal, and a reverse scissor bite is *not* the ideal in Pekingese. To adopt such a description could only mean a degeneration of the breed.

Controversial

The question of mouths has always been a controversial topic in Pekingese circles, no doubt partly due to the tradition of never opening up a mouth when judging the breed. I can go along with that provided one would also follow John Vlasto's advice and open a mouth when one considers it to be suspect.

The breed has had many dogs and bitches in the past, some well-known champions included, that have had weak chins, scissor bites if you like, and were even overshot. Some have been excellent producers recognized for their overall quality. One recognized the fact that they failed in strength of underjaw and were aware if one used them for breeding.

At times I have the impression that the tradition of not opening a Pekingese mouth is used as an excuse to cover up faults such as weak chins and narrow underjaws. If so, it would be better to start opening mouths to find out just how prevalent are the faults. It is senseless to ignore a mouth simply because tradition dictates it not be opened. Perhaps it is time for us to realize that ignorance is not necessarily bliss, and it is important to be wise when making any serious changes that can affect the future of the breed.

Can. Ch. St. Aubrey Ku Tinka of Elsdon, bred and owned by Nigel Aubrey-Jones and R. William Taylor, was a daughter of Am. & Can. Chik T'Sun of Caversham. When bred to Ch. Calartha Mandarin of Jehol, Ku Tinka produced Am. & Can. Ch. St. Aubrey Tinkabelle of Elsdon.

One of the author's favorite informal photographs of Tinkabelle, taken in September 1962.

6

The Blueprint of
the Pekingese Standard

SHOULD YOUR OWNERSHIP of the Pekingese extend beyond sharing your life with one or more of the breed entirely for companionship, and you should decide to become involved—no matter how fleetingly—in the exhibiting, breeding and maybe even judging of this most complex of breeds, it is essential that as much time as possible be devoted to reading and understanding the breed Standard. The previous chapter included the current Standard for the Pekingese in Great Britain and the United States. These two Standards differ slightly in phraseology, yet in essence they remain the same. But what is a breed Standard? In simple terms, the breed Standard is a written description of the perfect specimen of a breed. It outlines the ultimate in breed points, conformation and character. It is the blueprint to which all breeders should turn when attempting to improve their stock and to which all judges should refer when given the responsibility of assessing the breed in a competitive situation.

How Standards Developed

When the various breeds were evolving, fanciers gathered together to form breed clubs that aimed to foster the interests of the breed concerned. One of their earlier priorities was formulating a breed Standard because this would, in theory, be the most logical way to ensure future uniformity. If all breeders strove for the same goals, the breed would become more stable and less diverse.

In the cases of breeds that were developed to perform a specific job of work, such as Hounds, Gundogs and Terriers, their breed Standards were drawn up very much around purpose and function. There were sound, practical reasons that the various component parts of the animal were called for in the early breed Standards. Similarly with Non-Sporting breeds that were developed to guard, herd or hunt. Their Standards also relied almost exclusively on function for "breed characteristics."

Toys Are Different

However, the Toy breeds were not developed to protect their master or mistress, to hunt for food, herd cattle or locate game. Their sole purpose in life was to be companions—loyal, affectionate, healthy and also aesthetically pleasing to look at. Consequently the breed Standards found within the Toy Group (in breeds that are other than direct miniaturizations of an original, more functional breed) cannot always trace their requirements back to utilitarian purposes.

The breed Standards of Toys relate more usually to a man-made physique, soundness and health of mind and body, and eye appeal.

The Ideal Palace Dog

To appreciate the importance and significance of the Pekingese breed Standard, it should be realized that the Standards that exist today are based on a description of the *Ideal Palace Dog,* developed by the ancestors of Dowager Empress Tzu Hsi over many generations. Their challenge had been to breed a noble companion dog worthy of regal company and surroundings, and the "pearls" of description passed on by the Empress, though they might appear florid, verbose and archaic, should be studied by all Pekingese enthusiasts before they attempt to understand contemporary breed Standards.

The following, "dropped from the lips of Her Imperial Majesty, Tzu Hsi, Dowager Empress of the Flowery Land," may be regarded as one of the earliest breed Standards ever penned:

> Let the Lion Dog be small; let it wear the swelling cape of dignity around its neck; let it display the billowing standard of pomp above its back.
>
> Let its face be black; let its forefront be shaggy; let its forehead be straight and low, like unto the brow of an Imperial righteous harmony Boxer.
>
> Let its eyes be large and luminous; let its ears be set like the sails of a war-junk; let its nose be like that of the monkey god of the Hindus.
>
> Let its forelegs be bent so that it shall not desire to wander far or leave the Imperial precincts.
>
> Let its body be shaped like that of a hunting lion spying for its prey.
>
> Let its feet be tufted with plentiful hair that its footfall may be soundless; and for its standard of pomp let it rival the whisk of the Tibetan's yak, which is flourished to protect the Imperial litter from attacks of flying insects.
>
> Let it be lively that it may afford entertainment by its gambols; let it be timid that it may not involve itself in danger; let it be domestic in its habits that it may live

The Bugatti grandson, Am. & Can. Ch. St. Aubrey Goofus Brescia, seen winning Best of Breed on his American debut at the Philadelphia Kennel Club in 1967 under Ramona van Court; handled by Nigel Aubrey-Jones. Brescia was later sold to Mrs. Nathan Allen and Mildred Imrie.

Am. & Can. Ch. St. Aubrey Sun Burst of Elsdon pictured winning a Best of Breed under Diana Holman from England. Sired by Ch. St. Aubrey Dragonfly of Elsdon, Sun Burst was the result of a half brother to half sister mating, the common grandsire being Ch. St. Aubrey Laparata Dragon. He proved a most successful stud dog, siring among others Ch. Briarcourt Rule Britannia, who in turn produced the Westminster 1990 Best in Show winner, Ch. Wendessa Crown Prince. He is owned by Judy Bruckerhof.

in amity with other beasts, fishes or birds that find protection in the Imperial Palace. And for its color, let it be that of a lion—a golden sable, to be carried in the sleeve of a yellow robe, or the color of a red bear, or a black or white bear, or striped like a dragon, so that there may be dogs appropriate to every costume in the Imperial wardrobe.

Let it venerate its ancestors and deposit offerings in the Canine Cemetery of the Forbidden City on each new moon.

Let it comport itself with dignity; let it learn to bite the foreign devils instantly.

Let it be dainty in its food, and it shall be known for an Imperial dog by its fastidiousness.

Sharks' fins and curlews' livers and the breasts of quails, on these it may be fed; and for drink give it tea that is brewed from the spring buds of the shrub that groweth in the province of Hankow, or the milk of the antelopes that pasture in the Imperial parks. Thus shall it preserve its integrity and self-respect; and for the day of sickness, let it be anointed with the clarified fat of the leg of a sacred leopard, and give it to drink a throstle's egg shell full of the juice of the custard-apple in which has been dissolved three pinches of shredded rhinoceros horn, and apply to it piebald leeches. So shall it remain—but if it die, remember thou too art mortal.

Isn't that one of the most wonderful pieces of prose you have ever read? True, sharks' fins, curlews' livers, sacred leopards, rhinoceros horn and piebald leeches are not that commonplace today, so following the Empress's first-aid tips might prove a little difficult, but as for the remainder of her "pearls," I wonder whether our Pekingese would have changed that much had we retained her original "breed Standard."

So let us examine the American breed Standard item by item and try to understand as fully as possible what constitutes that impossible dream—the perfect Pekingese.

Expression

We are told that the expression of the Pekingese should suggest the Chinese origin in its quaintness and individuality, resemblance to the lion in directness and independence, and should imply courage, boldness, self-esteem and combativeness rather than prettiness, daintiness or delicacy.

Before we analyze the head in detail, we must try to come to grips with the Pekingese expression, for the expression is the first and last thing that hits any observer or judge. The Pekingese expression must convey its royal heritage. When a Pekingese gives you "the look," you *should* feel inferior. Look into the Pekingese eyes and sense the inscrutability, the defiance and the steady self-confidence that only this breed exudes. It is a quiet, knowing confidence, however, not the bouncy overpowering joie de vivre of the Poodle. This is the benign sagacity of the Mandarin.

Essential to the true Pekingese expression is correct eye position, shape and color, complementary ear placement, openness of features, finish of mouth and placement and width of nostrils—coupled, of course, with the essential shallowness of face, the straight and low forehead as required by the Empress.

118

Mary de Pledge's Ch. Ku-Jin of Caversham, which can be found in so many pedigrees on both sides of the Atlantic.

Am. & Can. Ch. St. Aubrey Singlewell Ku Donavan, imported by Nigel Aubrey-Jones and R. William Taylor, later the property of Nicholas Baker, Jr., of New York.

While the Pekingese is a Toy breed, it is not and never should be dainty, weedy or in any way lacking in strength and solidity. (Having said that, coarseness is something that should always be avoided.) When the expression of the Pekingese comes from a distinctly weak head, small and underdone in relation to the body, that strength and bearing can never be conveyed.

Head

Looking at the head in detail, we are told that the skull should be massive, broad, wide and flat between the ears and wide between the eyes, which should be large, dark, prominent, round and lustrous. The nose must be black, broad, very short and flat. The American Standard simply says "Stop—deep," while the ears need to be heart-shaped, not set too high, with leathers that are never long enough to come below the muzzle or carried erect, but rather drooping with long feather. The muzzle is described as being wrinkled, very short and broad, not overshot or pointed. A strong, broad underjaw is called for, with teeth that do not show.

Of course breed Standards are blueprints, and the publishers assume that the readers already know something about the subject. For example, omitted is the requirement for two eyes and four legs, but we all know dogs should be in possession of both. However, in the case of the American breed Standard (in the eyes of the breed expert), there may be rather too much taken for granted on behalf of the student.

The Pekingese is often described—maybe quite wrongly—as "a head breed," which would indicate the importance to be placed on the head, but personally I find myself becoming more concerned with the lack of understanding on the part of breeders and judges of the correct Pekingese construction and movement. Notwithstanding, the Pekingese head is the stamp of the breed, and no matter how wonderfully conformed a Pekingese is or how typically it moves, without a good enough head its progress will be minimal.

In Britain the phrase "envelope-shaped" was often used to describe the face of the Pekingese, to indicate that it should be wide and shallow, and framed with ear fringes that hang down at 90 degrees to the topskull. The topskull must be wide and flat. Domed skulls and apple-heads are alien to the breed and should be avoided when breeding, penalized when judging.

The requirement for a "prominent" eye can also be misleading. To some readers prominence might suggest a bolting eye (protruding with a fearful expression), maybe even combined with apparent white, which destroys the tranquility of expression that can be achieved only with a dark, round, full and yet in no way menacing eye.

The width between the eyes is also vitally important, for without sufficient width the face becomes crowded and lacks the desired openness. The nose leather ideally should be well up between the eyes in such a way that an imaginary line could be drawn between the center of the eyes and the top of the nose leather. The nose should, in fact, tilt slightly backward, and the nostrils should

Am. & Can. Ch. St. Aubrey Bumble Bee being handled by Nigel Aubrey-Jones. Bumble Bee was by Sunburst out of his half sister, both being by Dragonfly.

be wide and flared. Pinched nostrils are not only ugly and undesirable from a beauty standpoint, they are also detrimental to the dog's health and well-being.

Over the years there has been much discussion on the overnose wrinkle in the Pekingese, the broken wrinkle of earlier years now being much less common in favor of the complete wrinkle. The unexaggerated overnose wrinkle complements the Pekingese face beautifully, but a heavy, overdone wrinkle that tends to obscure the nose leather is another contributing factor toward creating a face that is less than open-featured.

Another point of the utmost importance in achieving the true "grotesqueness" of the ideal Pekingese expression is the correct strength of underjaw. This comes from a mouth that is considerably more undershot than that called for with the "reverse scissor bite" that the British Kennel Club was so keen to implement a few years ago. A wide, undershot lower jaw that also has a degree of depth is necessary in a face where the lips meet in a well-cushioned muzzle. Without sufficient strength of underjaw, an almost frog-like expression results, bland and lacking the "snooty" air of the real aristocrat.

Ear size has never been a great problem in the breed; the area where more shortcomings occur is in placement. Too high an ear set will cause flying ears that create a "startled" expression, while too low a set will give a houndy and rather somber expression.

With the present mania for hair, hair and more hair, one of the aspects of the Pekingese breed Standard that tends to warrant concern is the breed's body shape. The original breed Standard called for sufficient coat to enhance the body shape, not mask it entirely from view. The American Standard describes the body as being "heavy in front, well sprung ribs, broad chest, falling away lighter behind, lion-like, with back level. Not too long in body; allowance made for longer body in bitch."

Before progressing to the body, it is interesting to note that there is no mention of neck in the Standard, which is because the Pekingese has a very short neck, appearing shorter still with the mane of hair that adorns it. Far too many Pekingese today have too much neck, and this upsets the overall balance and bearing of the dog. "Necky" Pekingese are not wholly typical, and while they may appear "flashy" in Groups if carrying excess hair, please remember that the Pekingese is one breed where a great reach of neck is not an asset.

Structure and Movement

Returning to the body, imagine a concrete pear slung between the legs— not perched on top of them—and you are on your way toward understanding Pekingese shape. Correct body shape is vital if correct balance and movement are to be achieved. When you handle a Pekingese you should immediately be impressed with its great spring of rib and the relative lowness to ground of its torso. The rib cage should be low-slung, and any suggestion of a roach back (a prevalent fault and one that breeders do not find easy to eradicate) should be avoided. The backline should rise gently to the lighter loin that helps create this "pear-

Best in Show at Westminster 1990 was Edward B. Jenner's Ch. Wendessa Crown Prince, handled by Luc Boileau. Frank Sabella was the judge.

The Crown Prince grandson, Ch. Knolland Red Reuben, wins Best of Winners under Nigel Aubrey-Jones for owner Edward Jenner and handler Luc Boileau.

123

shaped'' body. When handling the body one should still get the impression of strength, firmness and fitness. There should be a solidness and great substance to the body, and Pekingese that appear narrow, boney or ''spidery'' underneath any amount of hair are not typical specimens of the breed.

While the Standard tells us the Pekingese should not be too long in body, it could also remind us that it should not be too short. Indeed, of the two failings, it could be argued that a Pekingese with a little extra length could still move with typical gait, yet a dog that is too short will have a ''proppy,'' almost Pom-like action, thus rendering the dog untypical. Certainly breeders would be well advised to be more forgiving of a little extra length than of an ultra-short Pekingese.

We now look at legs. The Standard calls for ''short forelegs, bones of forearm bowed, firm at shoulder, hind legs lighter, but firm and well-shaped.''

The Pekingese is beyond question one of, if not *the* most difficult breed to judge, and one of the areas where so much lack of understanding exists is in the front assembly. The large, well-sprung rib cage should rest snugly on the forelegs, which must be short. They should be *firm at the shoulder,* and the bones are bowed in such a way that the natural forehand stance gives stability and still creates the impression of width. The correct Pekingese gait can be achieved only with sound assemblies front and rear, the fore action being a smooth, fluid ''rolling'' one created by the body shape and the bow of the foreleg. Far too many judges in and outside the ring confuse gross unsoundness stemming from loose shoulders and anything-but-firm elbows as ''the Pekingese roll.''

Meanwhile, back at the hindquarters, our American Standard is of little help when it uses such a vague expression as ''well shaped.'' What is well shaped? Through the lightness of loin and comparative narrowness of the hindquarters in relationship to the forequarters, the hind legs will be correspondingly lighter in construction. If a Pekingese is correctly built, it will appear ''front heavy,'' with its center of gravity much nearer to its nose than its tail. To achieve the true Pekingese gait, the hindquarters will be moderately angulated (not as straight as the Chow Chow, not as angulated as the Beagle), firm and sound. As much as breeders would prefer not to acknowledge the fact (those breeders who know what a patella is, that is), slipping patellas do occur in the breed. To the inexpert eye they may be undetectable, but they constitute an unsoundness that can become firmly established and prove difficult to get rid of.

The construction of the hindquarters in the correctly structured Pekingese is such that the action when going away is close, almost scissorlike, yet still parallel, with no suggestion of hind legs plaiting or ''tripping over'' as the dog walks.

The unique combination of the true body shape, correctly constructed front and rear assemblies, impart to the Pekingese its true action. It is free, dignified and rolling—all wholly reminiscent of one of the Empress's junks in full sail.

At this juncture I must stress that correct Pekingese action, where it exists, can only be seen in a dog when gaited at a relatively slow speed. The speeds witnessed in our Group rings cannot possibly enable any judge to assess movement satisfactorily. Marathon paces may well be second nature to dogs with cubelike bodies and straight, long legs but are anathema to the correct Pekingese.

Great Pekingese move freely, with dignity and a bearing that can only be described as stately. Oftentimes speed can be assumed as merely hiding a multitude of sins.

On the subject of feet, the Standard requires them to be flat, with toes turned out, not round, and that the dog should stand well up on the feet, not the ankles.

This phraseology is very confusing. In essence the Standard is calling for a dog that is not down on its pasterns or generally weak in front, but at the same time we do not want a Pekingese that is "up on the feet" in the same sense as a Wire Fox Terrier or a Doberman. The Pekingese pasterns should be strong and firm shock absorbers, but not upright. "Upstanding," while being a treasured epithet in a large number of breeds, is not an adjective that the connoisseur of Pekingese would ever wish to have attributed to his dogs.

I have already discussed action since it is inseparable from body construction, and the American Standard's requirement for its being fearless, free and strong with a slight roll brings to light nothing that has not been discussed—other than, perhaps, temperament, which is ignored by our Standard.

Temperament

Temperament, disposition, character, personality, bearing—call it what you will—is what attracts different people to different breeds of dogs. The Pekingese breed Standard tells us very little about this and so assumes that we should all be credited with a great deal of imagination.

Other than merely mentioning its "fearless action," the Standard could well have gone on to say that the Pekingese should always be confident, courageous, brave, bold, defiant, plucky and independent—never uneasy, doubtful, nervous or anxious.

What has attracted and still attracts all of us to the Pekingese is the reputation it has earned for itself for being fearless, alert and intelligent. What has made us want to own a Pekingese is having met one of this breed that possessed all of these qualities. It is the character of the first Peke we met that impressed us—not the great spring of rib or the superb tail set! Let us not forget that, for many generations more than the majority of pure breeds to be found on the American Kennel Club's register, the Pekingese has been bred specifically to coexist with man. It was essential that its mental attitude and capacity was such that it could keep itself occupied and its royal cohabitants amused while resident in its native land. It needed to be resilient, bold, entertaining and yet obliging. Its heritage is such that the Pekingese has been "humanized" far more than any other breed, and this fact is no surprise to anyone who has ever lived with a Pekingese.

Temperament is a very precious part of the breed. If we think of the great Pekingese that have established mighty winning records on either side of the

Imported from England, Ch. St. Aubrey Cambaluc Lionhart was a son of the successful stud dog Ch. Jay Trump of Sunsalve. He is owned by Jane Henderson, who is rapidly collecting a team of top-winning Pekingese.

One of the latest imports from England by St. Aubrey-Elsdon is Can. Ch. Genisim Body Talk of St. Aubrey, bred by Jennifer Sims. He took Best of Winners at the 1989 Pekingese Club of America Summer Specialty.

Atlantic, we realize that they had this precious essential. For Pekingese to withstand the rigors of an exhibiting career and give their all in the show ring, moving with confidence and style, they must possess true Pekingese attitude. In this breed, possibly more than most, temperament directly affects physical appearance. The most exquisite Pekingese will be a nonstarter if its temperament is such that it drops its tail and shrinks away from competitors and judge. This is *not* the Lion Dog of Peking.

Without the mental makeup to complement the physical attributes, it is impossible to obtain the overall picture of this noble breed. Today there is much talk of unsoundness, but this talk tends to be confined to front legs or hind legs, and there is a temptation to forget that a sound mind is just as important as a sound body. In reality, a typical unsound dog is by far more desirable than a sound untypical one. We have all, at one time or another, stood at the ringside embarrassed for a fellow exhibitor leading a nervous, lethargic and uninterested specimen with its tail dragging behind it and its ears flying in every direction. This kind of display is usually the result of an unsound mind, no matter how many excuses to the contrary may be offered by the apologetic owner. Nervousness should never be tolerated in a Pekingese. It is a breed that should know no fear.

I make no excuse for reminding you at this point of the breed's original function, that of a companion dog. Toy dogs were bred to be pets. Many breeders would probably never admit to breeding ''pets'' because, sadly, this term has acquired derogatory overtones in exhibiting circles, but this is why the Pekingese came into being, and to fulfill its role as a companion animal, its soundness of mind is more important than its physical subtleties.

Ask yourself whether the Empress would have tolerated a downtailed, frightened Lion Dog more than one who had a slightly low tail set or weak chin?

Judges and exhibitors on both sides of the Atlantic are equally to blame for the problem of nervousness in the Pekingese today. As long as judges continue to accept and tolerate excuses made by exhibitors for nervous exhibits, the exhibitor will continue to breed and show them. All too often we hear, ''it must have been the long journey,'' ''he was scared by the vet,'' ''the Doberman in the crates on the way in screamed at him,'' and the endless list goes on. We are only deceiving ourselves if we accept this weakness in temperament and continue to breed to and from it.

The show ring (or, indeed, the whelping box) is no place for nervous or neurotic dogs. It is the shop window for the breed. It is not the place to lead-train puppies. It is a place where the exhibits should make the most of themselves, stand their ground and display all the virtues of the breed—physical and mental. Actors and actresses rehearse before they perform. If only in fairness to the dogs, they should be prepared and trained before they appear in the show ring. It is quite possible for an exceptionally good Pekingese puppy to be scared by a Great Dane and never raise his ''standard of pomp'' again. The reason for, or the cause of, the lack of good and correct temperament or true breed character should never be the concern of the judge. Faulty temperament should be penalized most severely. It is the only way it will be eliminated.

Coat

Now let us turn our attention to coat, in reality one of the most unimportant aspects of the Pekingese, being merely the "icing on the cake," yet one that has gotten totally out of proportion by many involved with the breed. The Standard calls for a coat that is "long with a thick undercoat, straight and flat, not curly, not wavy, rather coarse, but soft; feather on thighs, legs and toes long and profuse."

To the connoisseur of the breed, texture is far more important than abundance of coat. A Pekingese that appears short of coat and yet has the correct harsh top coat, coupled with the softer undercoat, is a far more worthwhile prospect than one that is dripping in endless coat, soft and woolly in texture, invariably lacking body of coat. As I mentioned earlier, the Pekingese coat should enhance its natural body shape, not mask it. Dogs that have hair sprouting out in all directions, creating a walking footstool, are not typical of the breed. Long fringes and trousers, profuse mane and sufficient body coat are all that is required of a beautiful Pekingese in the hairdressing stakes. But try telling that to some breeders! Study some of the early photographs in this book and really look into many of the turn-of-the-century dogs. Do they not have a beauty and honesty of their own, despite not being hampered by lengthy tresses?

Despite wanting more and more coat on their dogs' bodies, some Pekingese exhibitors seem determined to remove it elsewhere, thus going against the teachings of the breed's elders. For many years the long hair on the feet was highly prized, and the prospect of even tidying it up was unthinkable. I find some exhibitors cutting the hair back, especially on the forefeet, and while I find a little judicious thinning for hygiene's sake acceptable, merciless barbering of the forefeet creates what is, in my eyes, a hard and ugly picture that does nothing to enhance the overall glamour of the Pekingese.

The Standard is quite explicit on the mane, demanding that it be "profuse, extending beyond the shoulder blades, forming ruff or frill around the neck." Today many Pekingese lack a distinct mane because it merges with the body coat to form one mass of rather shapeless hair. Study photographs of some of the great champions of the past to see how handsome a fully-maned dog can look. The lavish mane, contrasting with the less profuse body coat, helped to create the leonine appearance of the breed. When moving, the mane settled back over the dog like billowing sails and contributed to the overall picture of correct shape.

Alas, the lack of contrast between mane and body coat, and the obsession with more and more of the latter, has meant that the coat pattern of many present-day Pekingese is far from the ideal called for in the breed Standard.

Color

The breed Standard is indeed a generous one where color is concerned. All colors are allowed by the American Pekingese Standard, though its British counterpart has long outlawed albino and liver—in my opinion, correctly so.

The well-known judge and author Anna Katherine Nicholas admires one of her winners, a white owned by Mr. and Mrs. Peter Shoemaker of the Cumlaude Kennel.

Listed colors include red, fawn, black, black and tan, sable, brindle, white and parti-color well defined; black masks and spectacles are called for around the eyes in the American Standard, with lines to the ear being desirable.

While some breeders may find the more fundamental aspects of the breed Standard difficult to fully comprehend, it has been my experience that they very often have fixed ideas on color. The question of color could be dismissed by simply quoting the Standard: "All colors are allowable." Having said that, human frailties and personal preferences have always played a part in the direction color should take in this breed. Students of Pekingese art will be well aware that most of the early works in which Pekingese were featured depicted dogs of the parti-colored coat pattern. Yet when the Pekingese first arrived in England, the pioneer breeders expressed a preference in no uncertain terms for rich reds with black masks and tips. They were mainly led by Lady Algernon Gordon-Lennox, who founded the immortal Goodwood strain; she maintained that the original Palace imports were of this color and therefore this should be the color to aim for. Indeed, when she and her husband judged, much attention was given to rewarding their favorite color.

Their theory falls down, however, when we look at pictures of Looty, which was a very obvious parti-color. Those who chose to differ with Lady Gordon-Lennox believed that if the reds were so highly prized, it was unlikely they would have been left behind to fall into the hands of "the foreign devils," and suggested that these were therefore the least valued of the colors.

Come what may, history and evolution have preserved a rainbow of colors in the Pekingese, and we each have our personal preferences. However, when judging the breed, color should be of little consequence. What matters are type, soundness, balance, movement, character and quality. A good dog is never a bad color.

Numerically speaking, fawns and their variations have dominated the show ring, but there remain ardent devotees of "the colors" (by which is traditionally meant whites, blacks, black and tans and parti-colors) who will ensure that they never die out.

There exists a danger, however, when breeding the less popular colors that the color itself becomes the major consideration and this takes priority over type and other essentials. The baby tends to be thrown out with the bath water.

In evaluating a specimen of "the colors" in the show ring, our criterion should not be "it's good for a white/black/parti, and so forth," but "it's good for a Pekingese."

The magnanimity of the breed Standard allows us to indulge our personal fads and fancies with a myriad of colors, each of which is equally correct, but we should not allow personal preferences to drift into textbooks and become confused with essentials.

Unlike the British Standard, the American version calls for a black mask and spectacles around the eyes. The spectacles, so-called because paler hairs in the darker facial coat create this impression, are seldom seen nowadays. The current fashion is for some judges to pass by a beautiful Pekingese unless it has

The parti-colored Pekingese has a devoted following of enthusiasts, one being Patty Davis of San Diego, California, who owns these three very even black-and-whites.

a solid black mask extending the full depth of the face. Yet in truth a black muzzle complemented with black eye framing will produce a much more "alive" expression than the totally jet black face in which there is no relief at all.

Pigment

While discussing color it is pertinent to mention pigment, a much more important requirement. Regardless of coat color, the Pekingese should always have dense, definite pigment. Good pigment is essential in both the show ring and whelping box. Occasionally one finds weak pigment manifested in a bluish or pinkish hue over the muzzle, usually coupled with lack of black in eye rims and on foot pads. Weak pigment is a fault that can plague a breeder for generations and therefore should be avoided at all costs. Lack of pigment should not be confused with lack of black hair. A Pekingese can have a self-colored face and still have excellent pigment. Pigment is found in the skin rather than the coat.

Tail

One of the most important features of any breed when it comes to completing the overall picture and "finish" is the tail or, to be more specific, the tail set and carriage. The Pekingese's "standard of pomp" is no less important. In the first place, tail carriage is indicative of temperament and attitude and therefore tells us a lot about the dog's character. Furthermore, the set of the tail and the manner in which it is held contribute greatly to the outline and balance of the Pekingese. The Standard requires the tail to be set on high, lying well over the back to either side and having long, profuse, straight feather.

A tail that is low set will detract from the whole rear assembly and is invariably coupled with weak hindquarters, producing a stilted, almost shuffling hind movement. Logically, too, a low-set tail will create the impression of additional length of back. Seldom will a Pekingese have a too-high tail set, but carriage is important. A tail lacking the required overback carriage, creating an ugly "jug handle" appearance, can only detract from the dog's overall outline.

The gentle curve of the correct Pekingese tail should not be confused with the much tighter curled tail of the Pug. A tail so tightly curled that its end points backward rather than forward will produce an untypical "chrysanthemum" effect, again detracting from the clean and gentle outline we should be looking for.

The tail may be considered a minor detail by some, but it serves to give us a great insight into the dog as a whole, and as such its importance should never be underestimated.

Size

We now come to one of the most sensitive areas of the breed Standard—size. Here the American and British Standards differ considerably; the U.S. blueprint says "being a Toy Dog, medium-size preferred, providing type and

Two enchanting miniatures: Copplestone Mr. Pinkcoat (left) and his exquisite sister, Copplestone Miss Pinkcoat, who were obtained by Betty Shoemaker from Yvonne Bentinck.

The legendary Binkie—popular columnist and long-serving companion to the author.

points are not sacrificed; extreme limit fourteen pounds." (Note, too, that a dog over fourteen pounds is listed as a disqualifying fault). The British Standard calls for "the ideal weight not exceeding eleven pounds for dogs and twelve pounds for bitches. The dog should look small but be surprisingly heavy when picked up. Heavy bone and a sturdy, well-built body are essentials of the breed."

For some years it has been assumed that American dogs are much larger than British dogs, yet some of the most memorable of American dogs have fallen well within the British limits. The most important thing to remember is that the Pekingese should be *multum in parvo*—much in little. The Pekingese should look small, yet when handled the weight should be surprisingly greater than anticipated. It should be remembered that a large dog that picks up light should never beat an otherwise equal small dog that picks up heavy. The Pekingese must have bone and substance, and the ratio of weight to size is of much greater importance than either weight or size in isolation. It is no good claiming to like dogs of nine pounds and admire equally a small, low, heavy-boned dog of that weight as much as a taller, finer-boned, narrower dog of the same weight.

Since the emphasis in the United States seems to center around Group and Best in Show wins, with the larger proportion of judging being performed by nonspecialist judges, there may exist a belief that a little extra size (coupled with the inevitable extra hair!) will make a dog appear more "impressive"; however, I can assure you that some of the most impressive Pekingese I have known would have been described as "small," but within that smallness of frame existed a wealth of substance that contributed to their greatness in no small measure.

"Size"—in the sense of height, width and length—is not the important factor when assessing a Pekingese. It is the relative weight and substance to that size that matter. Pick up a Pekingese. If it is surprisingly heavy and falls within the weight limits of the Standard, its size is acceptable.

From a breeder's point of view it is generally accepted that the larger— dare I say coarser—and more masculine a bitch is, the better prospect as a brood bitch. But this is a sweeping generalization that does not necessarily hold water. I have known many judges to heap awards on "dual-purpose" size bitches over smaller bitches of superior quality, in the assumption that they will reproduce more easily, only to discover the contrary. No judge can predict how good a producer a bitch will become. What is important is general structure rather than "size."

There also exists within the fancy a group of breeders who openly advocate smaller, refined males and stronger, larger females as the recipe for success. Again, this cannot be proved conclusively in a breed with as many complexities as the Pekingese.

Probably the most likely brood bitches are those that have "the body of a truck driver and the face of a lady"!

The expression "sleeve dog" is one often heard within Pekingese circles; it comes from the Chinese tradition of carrying smaller Pekingese in the sleeves of their robes. Britain has its own Sleeve Dog Club that aims to foster the interests of the sleeve; the term today is taken to refer to Pekingese that weigh up

An outstanding example of an under-six-pound "sleeve," St. Aubrey Red Marquis of Pekehuis, owned by Nigel Aubrey-Jones and R. William Taylor. A Best in Show winner at the Pekingese Sleeve Dog Club's show in England.

Ti Toi and Mai Toi II won seventeen Best Brace in Show awards for Betty Shoemaker. They weighed four and a half pounds each.

Can. Ch. St. Aubrey Dragonfly of Elsdon; photograph of a painting by Cherie Williamson Rush. Dragonfly typifies what the St. Aubrey-Elsdon Kennel strives to breed: a short, compact and thickset dog that picks up surprisingly heavy for its size. He was a most successful stud dog, and litter brother to the Westminster Best in Show winning bitch, Am. & Can. Ch. St. Aubrey Dragonora of Elsdon. Sired by the great Dragon, Dragonfly had a short but successful show career in Canada where he was allbreed Best in Show. In the United States he was shown twice and was Best of Winners at two consecutive Pekingese Club of America Summer Specialties for a total of ten points . . . an uncrowned champion!

to seven pounds. My early memories were of a time when sleeve dogs weighed no more than six pounds, and miniatures weighed up to seven.

The sleeve is something of a subculture within the Pekingese fancy, and there are many who would not survive without one as a personal companion. The true sleeve is every bit as solid and substantial as its larger brothers and sisters but scaled down proportionately. Please do not think that staying within the weight limits by virtue of lacking bone and body renders a small dog a sleeve. It does not. The true sleeve is sturdy and every bit as tough as any standard weight and is not as delicate as some people would have you believe. They are also very long-lived. For many years a personality-plus sleeve by the name of Binkie shared my life. She found dog shows beneath her, yet in her own right she became a famed columnist of the canine world and left me for better things when she was in her fifteenth year.

It is generally considered that sleeves cannot compete on equal terms with standard-weight dogs, yet several have proved that this is not the case, particularly in Britain. As an example of an exquisite sleeve, study the photograph of Copplestone Miss Pinkcoat, imported by Mrs. Shoemaker. She was a perfect Pekingese in miniature.

Evaluating Faults

The American Standard says that the following faults should be penalized: protruding tongue, badly blemished eyes, overshot mouths and wry mouths.

A protruding tongue does not need explanation. Neither do badly blemished eyes. Concerning mouths, the overshot mouth is one in which the incisors of the upper jaw protrude beyond those of the lower. It is often accompanied by a weakness of underjaw and lack of chin, consequently denying the dog the classic Pekingese expression.

It is surprising how many different interpretations of the "wry mouth" I have heard over the years. A wry mouth results when the lower jaw is set at an angle to the upper jaw, giving the finish of mouth a "crooked" or "askew" appearance. On closer inspection the lower incisors are not parallel with the upper, so that the distance between the upper and lower teeth at one side of the mouth is not the same as that between the upper and lower teeth at the other side. The wry mouth is a fault that is not easily gotten rid of in a breeding program and should not be encouraged.

In the American Standard there are only two disqualifications: a dudley nose and weight over fourteen pounds. A dudley nose is one that is not fully pigmented so there are areas of pink on the actual nose leather. It should be remembered that sometimes a puppy will be slow in filling in, so maybe a little tolerance could be shown when the lack of pigment is slight and the subject a young specimen.

Whether it be to the breeder, the handler or the judge, the Pekingese presents a great challenge. In a breed where so many features are "unnatural"—shortened foreface, bowed forelegs and so forth—breeding type is far from easy.

The Importance of Judging

Judging the breed well is difficult enough for those who have firsthand experience of it, so imagine the challenge it must be to someone who has only the breed Standard to go by.

Much as the word pictures of the Standard may try to convey the perfect specimen to the reader, the component parts can make sense only when an outstanding dog is encountered in the flesh. One day in your career as a judge you will suddenly stumble across a Pekingese whose magnificent, large, expressive head fits snugly onto its shapely, solid body. Its tail carriage and overall demeanor will convey its Imperial heritage, and its coat will add glamour and style to the dog within. When it walks it is with dignity and confidence, and its overall quality is such that your eye is drawn to its total self—not its head, its coat or its movement—because its virtues are so well balanced that no one overshadows another. When you meet such a Pekingese, savor the moment. Study it in all its glory, for you have met a great one, and those years of studying the breed Standard and searching for perfection will suddenly fall into place. You are now beginning to understand the Pekingese.

While discussing the breed Standard, it is appropriate to mention approaches to judging. The very invitation to judge a breed is an honor, an honor that should have been earned—either by breeding and exhibiting high-quality Pekingese with some consistency in the case of the breeder-judge, or by having established a reputation for judging other breeds knowledgeably and without fear or favor, in the case of the all-breed or multi-breed judge.

Judging is all about finding the best dog on the day and rewarding it. It is not a platform for settling old scores or becoming involved in politics. Dogs must be judged on their physical attributes as seen by the judge, regardless of winning records and elaborate promotion. Judging is difficult enough without a judge giving a second thought to these irrelevancies.

Judging is about putting *up* great dogs because of virtues and not putting them *down* because of their faults. The greatest dogs I have known have had their imperfections. Their greatness stemmed from the harmonious blending together of many virtues that, in a very positive manner, more than outweighed any minor blemishes.

More important to the judge than finding out what is wrong with a Pekingese is finding out what is right with it. Judging is a balancing act in which faults and virtues should always be seen in perspective, with the emphasis being on the whole picture created by the component parts.

The breed Standard for the Pekingese is quite elastic in some of its demands and, rightly so, lacking in some meticulous detail. We therefore have a Standard that allows for a variation of types to fit into its framework without having to stray unduly far from it. Judges, like breeders, have types they prefer.

My personal preference is for a short, thickset body with a high tail set, giving a complete picture of a dog that has some degree of shape, at the same time appearing to be all in one piece. It is for this very reason that I have always

St. Aubrey Divine of Elsdon was sired by the Mayfly son, French & Can. Ch. St. Aubrey Jim Brady of Elsdon, and is now owned by Allan Taylor and Idris Jones in the United Kingdom, famous for their Belroyd Pembroke Welsh Corgi kennel.

Am. & Can. Ch. St. Aubrey Gadfly of Elsdon, full brother to Toyboy and Bar Fly; owned by Nigel Aubrey-Jones.

138

liked to see Pekingese walk freely around a ring where they can display an outline and very clearly give an overall picture of whether they are too long and shapeless, and whether their heads are the correct size and carried on the correct short neck.

Having seen the whole picture in profile and in motion, coming and going, I feel the eye has been educated to know just where to place the hands when going over the dog. We constantly hear that an abundance of coat can hide a multitude of sins, yet it would be as well to bear in mind that, to the knowledgeable and experienced eye, an abundance of coat of the wrong texture can also reveal a similar number of sins!

Long-coated dogs have to be handled to have their true merit correctly evaluated, and sufficient time must be spent on the table getting to the basics of every Pekingese you judge.

The judging of the specialist versus the all-arounder (all-breed judge) and the influence each has on a breed is constantly discussed. An important point that might be missed is that, regardless of who judges, it should be good. There is a need for both opinions in every breed to keep it healthy and free from personal prejudices, and there should not be any great difference of opinion regarding the basic essentials in any breed. If we take a good look at the records of many top-winning dogs, we will see that in the majority of cases they have been rewarded by both types of judges. It also tends to make us think that there is a lot more smoke than real fire in the stories about judging being either very good or very bad.

It is possible for a specialist to have a great knowledge of a breed and be able to discuss and write about it with great conviction, but when he walks into the center of the ring, it all deserts him. He cannot make definite decisions in assessing relative merits and demerits. He becomes hesitant and confused, and he can make a hopeless mess of judging—but the knowledge of the breed still remains with him. Specialist or all-rounder, a judge needs knowledge, integrity, experience and the strength of character to be able to apply his knowledge of the breed in the correct perspective and never to be more impressed with the exhibitor than the exhibit.

There are many who believe that it is much easier for an all-arounder to gain knowledge of a breed than for the specialist to acquire the strength of character and the ability to demonstrate his knowledge of the breed in the center of the ring. It is an established fact that good judges are always searching for knowledge, and the most important achievement for any type of judge is that he or she does the job well. Any judge worth his or her salt can decide whether he or she has done this.

A V.I.P.-bred puppy owned by Patty Davis poses as only a Pekingese can.

7

Breeding Pekingese and Selecting a Puppy for the Show Ring

T HE BREEDING of any livestock can be a most heartbreaking affair, with all the disappointments it can present. Genuine breeders have to be really dedicated to take this all in their stride and try, try, try again! Those who have been fortunate enough to travel and meet some of the great breeders of the past and of today are lucky. To hear of their experiences and see some of the results of their breeding theories can prove to be invaluable. It also proves that our impatience is not always justified.

Laying the Groundwork

Some people seem to have a knack or gift in being able to produce top dogs. They make it appear very easy, but the careful study of pedigrees created by the successful breeder will prove that there was a pattern, an idea and a goal in mind before the final results were achieved. The great thrill and excitement of breeding a great dog that makes a great impact on the breed is something unique and tremendously satisfying. Unfortunately, it is something shared by only a few in every breed, but it is from this faction of the fancy that we look for our authorities. This is where knowledge, backed by experience, is truly reliable.

Breeding Pekingese is not for the fainthearted. It is probably the most difficult of all breeds to produce consistently.

Few people buy their first Pekingese with a view to establishing a kennel. Most start off with a pet, having been impressed by the charms of another companion dog; one Pekingese leads to two, then three and gradually the pet owner becomes a breed enthusiast, then drifts into becoming "a breeder."

Several years of hard work and heartache can be saved by looking dispassionately at your original dogs, and to do so you must know something about the breed. Read as much as is available, go to dog shows, study top dogs and talk to successful breeders. Get fixed in your mind's eye the sort of Pekingese you want to breed. It is hoped that that mental ideal will meet the requirements of the breed Standard.

Choosing Foundation Stock

If you already have a bitch, assess her physically and then look at her pedigree. It could be that she has a few minor flaws that would prevent her from going to the very top in the show ring, but if she is of good basic type, substantial and sound, and has a pedigree of some consequence, then she could prove a worthwhile foundation.

If you feel that your original bitch lacks basic merit and is of insignificant breeding, it is wiser to retain her as a companion and go out specifically to buy a more suitable foundation. It makes sense to buy something from the lines you most admire and, if possible, find a bitch that is linebred; in other words, that has a pedigree in which the same dogs or families will be found more than once. A pedigree in which no dog appears more than once in five generations may well produce "hybrid vigor," but the type she will produce will be just a matter of guesswork.

For example, if you particularly admire Champion So-So and many of its offspring have also impressed you, try to find a bitch that is linebred to him—maybe from a litter sired by a So-So son out of a So-So daughter; maybe sired by So-So out of his own granddaughter. Starting off with a bitch from this kind of combination means that your foundation will, if bred sensibly, breed dogs for you that resemble So-So in general type.

Speak to as many breeders with experience and success as possible, and find out everything you can about So-So, its parents, grandparents and siblings. You will hear conflicting stories, and here you must use common sense. If nine out of ten people tell you that So-So had wondrous dark eyes but one insists its eyes were yellow, the chances are it is because on one memorable occasion that particular person's Ping-Pong was beaten by So-So for the breed!

Remember that, beautiful as So-So was, it probably had some faults or other in its family background. Find out what they were and bear them in mind when you come to breed your So-So offspring. Doubling up on faults that lie dormant on both sides of a breeding can ingrain them in your stock for good. Research your pedigrees thoroughly.

Someone once said, "The best way to produce good-looking babies is to breed good-looking girls to good-looking boys"; there is much sense in that

Am. & Can. Ch. St. Aubrey Tinkabelle of Elsdon pictured winning Best Bitch at the Pekingese Club of America Summer Specialty in 1962 under the famous Pekingese judge and authority John B. Royce, himself owner of the Dah Lyn Pekingese Kennel in Massachusetts. Tinkabelle went on to Best of Breed at the 1963 Summer Specialty and Best Bitch again at the 1964 Specialty. Her record of three consecutive Best Bitch awards at the Summer Specialty was equaled only by another St. Aubrey-Elsdon-bred bitch, Anne Snelling's Am. & Can. Ch. St. Aubrey Dragonora of Elsdon.

statement. It is unlikely that breeding a poor bitch to a poor male will give you lovely puppies; and in the unlikely event of this happening, when they in turn are bred, you can wager that they will not reproduce their own quality.

The best kind of foundation bitch is sound, solid, substantial, totally typical with no glaring faults and not too small.

Selecting the Stud

When it comes to breeding your bitch, look for a stud dog that is of similar basic type and that shares with the bitch a common ancestry of quality. Much nonsense is talked about "linebreeding," and very few people today understand the term. I laughingly hear of the "Bugatti line." I once owned Ch. Goofus Bugatti, a beautiful dog, but there is no such thing as "the Bugatti line," merely descendants of Bugatti—and distant ones at that.

The stud dogs most likely to prove valuable are those that carry high-quality, good-producing dogs several times in their pedigree; these dogs all possess a certain consistency of quality and type.

To illustrate the point, I make no apologies for citing Ch. St. Aubrey Laparata Dragon, which has contributed so much to the breed in this country. He transmitted his many qualities and, when linebred, the virtues of Dragon still manifested themselves. But why was he such a good producer?

Ch. Caversham Ku Ku of Yam was not only a great winner in England, he was considered by many eminent authorities the most outstanding Pekingese ever bred. He also had the ability to pass on his type. Dragon was from a breeding of a half sister to a half brother, both parents being out of a bitch whose sire was Eng. Ch. Cherangani Chips. Chips was a great little dog that exuded quality and classic type from within his small frame. His grandsires were Ch. Ku Jin of Caversham and Ch. Goofus Le Grisbie, both of which were by the immortal Ku Ku.

You will see that already Dragon had the makings of a stud dog, yet his background was enhanced by the fact that the two dogs to whom his double granddam had been bred to produce his parents were both out of bitches descended at least twice from Ku Ku. In fact, Dragon traced back six generations in direct male line to Ku Ku, every link in the chain being a British champion.

It is essential to be able to read and appreciate a pedigree before you embark on breeding your bitch. Becoming a breeder in the true sense of the word involves a good deal more than shipping your bitch to a dog you have never seen who happens to be topping the ratings.

Having settled on the dog you wish to use, contact its owner and ask for the owner's opinion of the proposed mating. The owner may, if he has the breed's welfare at heart, confide that this is not the right mating for your bitch and explain why. If it makes sense, be guided by the owner and think again.

Having agreed with the owner on the choice of a stud dog, it would be courteous to advise when your bitch is expected in season—not that many Pekingese ladies obligingly begin their seasons regularly every six months!

Am. & Can. Ch. St. Aubrey Whispers of Elsdon, daughter of Bees Wing and Gossip, owned by Mrs. Sidney Domina.

Ch. St. Aubrey Bar Fly of Elsdon was a full brother to Toyboy. He is now owned by Dr. Passiri Nisalak and Mrs. Kanchanarak Charoenchai of Bangkok.

In Britain, where distances are so small, breeding a bitch is a relatively simple matter. Arrangements are made by phone, the bitch is driven to the dog, serviced and driven home. In the United States it is not quite that simple. Since the country is vast and air travel is routine, the chances are good that the stud of your choice may well be off on circuit and not due home for several days after your bitch is ready for servicing.

Arrangements should be made with the stud dog owner to the maximum satisfaction of all parties, and the bitch duly bred. Bitches vary considerably as to the right day for them to be bred. Some breeders tell you the ninth, eleventh or thirteenth day is the right one, but in my experience Mother Nature is the best indicator. If you are running a kennel and have a male of your own, the bitch will flirt shamelessly, flagging her tail to one side and advertising her delicate state when she is ready. I have found that the day after a bitch stops showing color in her discharge is often the right day. By checking her daily with cotton or a facial tissue, you will detect when the bright red discharge pales and then loses color. This is a good guideline.

As to the breeding itself, place yourself in the hands of the stud dog owner—not literally!—because the breed is notoriously uncooperative to mate, and an experienced hand is necessary. The stud owner may ask you to leave the bitch for the actual mating. This may be advisable since the owner's presence may distract her. Few serious stud owners, however, would object to your seeing the bitch once she has "tied" with the dog; this is advisable to ensure that you have had the services of the stud of your choice!

Care of the In-Whelp Bitch

More harm than good is done by feeding supplements and additives to the pregnant bitch. If she is receiving a well-balanced diet, she should not need any supplementation until after whelping.

The average gestation period is sixty-three days, but don't assume that all bitches whelp to order. Your bitch should be introduced to her whelping quarters from the fiftieth day so that she has time to get used to the new surroundings that should afford her quiet and seclusion.

When your bitch approaches whelping time, she will appear restless and agitated, and this may be the time to alert your veterinarian, just in case you require professional assistance.

You should always research the whelping history behind your bitch. Find out whether or not the bitches behind her whelped naturally or if there is a history of Caesarean sections. Bitches from free-whelping lines are more likely to self-whelp than bitches from lines that necessitate a high percentage of Caesareans.

Whelping Hints

Once your bitch starts labor, whelping should progress naturally. Personally, I would not allow a bitch to strain for more than two hours before seeking veterinary intervention. On the birth of the first puppy, the bitch should try to

Two Cumlaude puppies, linebred by Betty Shoemaker for color.

clean it up as best as she can, but you may need to help. She may not have cut the umbilical cord herself, so this could need clamping with hemostats and manual cutting. In the event of the afterbirth not coming away naturally, the bitch should be monitored closely because she might eat the afterbirth—a quite natural process. After whelping, your veterinarian might recommend a shot of Pituitrin to cleanse the bitch of any retained afterbirths. I cannot emphasize strongly enough the importance of a veterinarian who has experience with Toy breeds and whom you trust.

In my experience, bitches do better having puppies removed, dried and got going manually, and placed on a heated pad in a separate box until the entire whelping is over. This means she is not distracted by existing puppies when trying to give birth. The labor over, she is presented with her entire litter—cleaned, strong and healthy.

Weaning

We begin weaning at three weeks of age with scraped raw beef and give goat's milk rather than cow's. Feeding is very much a personal thing, and the feeding regime you choose to adopt for your Pekingese will be entirely a matter of personal preference. These days there are so many different feeding systems available that breeders are spoiled for choice, and the ultimate method will probably develop through a trial-and-error process.

From Whelping Box to Winners' Circle

This book is not aimed at those who have just bought their first Pekingese, so I must assume that you already know how to feed and rear the puppies. What you might not know is how to select from the first litter the best prospect for the show ring, so let us look at "sorting out" the litter in the search for that future star.

Even when the puppies are learning to walk, you will be able to gain a valuable insight into their future "attitude" in the show ring. Some puppies are bold and cheeky, their tails never down, and keen to show their littermates who is boss! Others are more reluctant to show off their virtues. At the earliest stage it is important that your puppies get used to all kinds of strange noises and sights—this is character building.

When it comes to the physical attributes you should look for in your eight-week-old Pekingese puppy, the first priority is that it should stand and walk on four good legs, and be well boned and sturdy so that when it stands naturally there is no looseness in front and no weakness behind. It should have poise, style and arrogance despite its gross immaturity. Its tail set should be high and its carriage over the back, not curling backward, and above all, your show puppy should be compact—not long and stringy but more "chunky," with the promise of a good spring of rib. The head should be wide and shallow, the features well laid out and the nostrils open—indeed a smaller version of the adult head.

148

This photograph illustrates beautifully the sort of forehand to look for in a future show winner. These three grew up to be (left to right): Can. Ch. St Aubrey Zara of Elsdon (dam of Ch. St. Aubrey Gadfly of Elsdon), St. Aubrey Jim Dandy of Elsdon (owned by Mr. and Mrs. de Wilde in Belgium, where he is a big winner), and St. Aubrey Zuchini of Elsdon (now in France, where he is a CACIB winner for Messrs. Finer and Swirskey).

Can. Ch. St. Aubrey Mugiechun Maybell, owned by R. William Taylor, is a granddaughter of both Mayfly and Dragonfly and has produced Divine, among others.

If you are setting up a kennel, do not dismiss a well-constructed, confident, compact bitch because she might have a less than classic head. She could be valuable as a breeding bitch, so don't be keen to move her on. A male of similar quality is another matter. Breeders have at their disposal, broadly speaking, the cream of the stud dogs throughout the country, so it is unlikely that they will be interested in using something of yours if it is less than top quality.

It is essential that you are as critical as possible of your own stock if you are to make a success of breeding Pekingese. Do not see your geese as swans.

The "Top" Stud Dog

It would appear from the records that there is some reluctance on the part of breeders to take full advantage of the top studs available to them. However, before discussing this matter, we should first establish exactly what constitutes a top stud dog.

Is a good stud a dog that produces a number of mediocre champions that never do much more than simply gain their titles and end their impression there? Or is a good stud dog one that sires a few successful show dogs that win top awards in both Group and Best in Show competition, and figure regularly in the pedigrees of many other show dogs, and bitches that regularly produce exceptional champions?

The first-mentioned type of stud dog can quickly and easily have his reputation as a sire publicized and enhanced by big kennels that can quickly pilot dogs through to their titles. The second kind, however, is the one that makes the most important and favorable impression on the breed.

The term "stud dog" is to my way of thinking one of the most abused terms of description in the fancy. So often a small breeder with one or two bitches purchases an ordinary dog just to produce puppies regardless of quality and then gives this ordinary dog the title of stud dog. This type of dog costs far more—in more ways than one—than the price of several stud services to a top producing stud dog in the real sense.

Consider the cost of either breeding or importing a top stud dog. Purchase price, show expenses and advertising can run into several thousands of dollars, yet the services of some top-caliber studs are available for a few hundred dollars. It would appear that the stud fees of the top dogs are well within the reach of every breeder. If not, they should not be breeding dogs because it costs money to breed good dogs, and those are the only kind we should be aiming to produce.

It would make interesting reading if we had the information as to the number of bitches that some dogs have bred and what they had produced. Some have bred as little as six in one year and produced stock that has made a favorable impression from coast to coast. There are others, however, that have bred upward of twenty bitches in a year and produced very few that have made any impression. The dog that is mated to fewer and produced better is without question the more important stud.

In studying the history of the breed, it can easily be seen that the most

Mrs. Walter M. Jeffords's Chico of Chinatown at nine months of age demonstrates Pekingese shape; note the massive head, high tail set and short, well-boned forelegs. In maturity Ch. Chico was a Best in Show winner at the Pekingese Club of America Specialty for American-breds.

Ch. St. Aubrey Bees Wing of Elsdon pictured as a puppy. His stance, expression, shape and overall balance were in evidence at a very early age. The property of Edward B. Jenner, he became one of the leading Pekingese winners in the United States.

151

Arlon D. Duit's Rodari the Dragon at Lon Du, pictured at his first show as a puppy, winning Best in Sweepstakes under Carol Hollands.

Ch. Sunburst Moon Rock, a son of Eng. & Am. Ch. Changkim Moon River, winning with breeder-owner-handler Karen Schultz under Richard Thomas. Edna Voyles presents the trophy.

successful breeders have always used the best studs available. They realized that good breeding just does not happen. It takes years to establish the consistent benefits of good breeding, but it has been proved so often and is still being proved that only well-planned breedings produce good dogs. A top-winning show dog need not necessarily be a successful stud dog. Rushing to breed to the top-winning dog is not breeding to the top producing stud. In many cases it is the sire of the top winner that constitutes a stud dog.

Linebreeding has almost always played a very important part in the success of most top stud dogs and has been most rewarding to breeders in the past. Present-day records seem to indicate that the same is true today. A study of the background of some famous strains can reveal many interesting facts. Unfortunately it is difficult today to establish a real "strain" because this requires a fairly large kennel, and today's economy hardly encourages that. No kennel can be founded on a haphazard breeding program. It is important to study pedigree to see which matings for several generations led to producing the great ones. Every breeding is important; as we have seen, the result of just one breeding can change the whole pattern of the breed.

The choice of a stud dog is a serious matter; it deserves a great deal of thought that no serious breeder can afford to ignore. Every litter presents a new problem and another headache, and even when the ultimate in perfection has been bred, the genuine breeder will always ask, "Now who should I breed this to . . .?"

Two top-class puppies sired by Eng. Ch. St. Aubrey Carnival Music of Eastfield out of a daughter of Ch. Goofus Bugatti.

It is advisable to get Pekingese puppies used to regular grooming from an early age. Here two youngsters prepare themselves for beauty-parlor treatment with their favorite coat dressing!

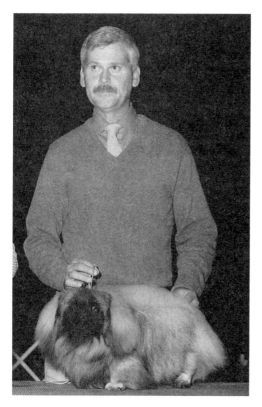

Warcrest's Fu Yong Talisman, handled by co-owner Malcolm Moore. Talisman was the sire of Ch. Merrimac's Andreas Silbermann.

8

Grooming the Pekingese

ONE OF THE GLORIES of the Pekingese—and indeed of any long-haired breed—is its coat, and unless you are prepared to spend time on its grooming, you would be better off with a smooth-coated breed.

Training the Puppy

The first essential is to get your Pekingese puppy used to standing on a table, preferably with a suitably light leash around its neck. This routine should be started at about eight weeks of age. At the same age or even earlier you should get the puppy used to lying on its back, to make grooming the underparts as easy as possible. The best way to begin this is by turning the puppy over on your lap, if only for a tummy-tickling session initially! First off, the overturning and table-standing should be nothing more than a confidence-building exercise and last just a few minutes each day. Once your puppy has accepted these as part of its daily routine, you can begin grooming in earnest.

Hygiene Essentials

Basic hygiene is an integral part of grooming, and to this end your puppy should be cleaned every time it has been out to relieve itself. From an early age it is advisable to scissor away carefully any soiled hair from around the anus and, in the case of male puppies, from the end of the sheath. All this attention will help toward personal cleanliness and avoid staining.

The Pekingese face requires special attention. Its structure is such that the skin concealed by the overnose wrinkle needs to be kept dry so that moisture does not build up. This will result initially in an unpleasant odor and could later lead to infection. Twice daily, using a cotton ball, clean this area well and also around the eyes, which may water a little from time to time.

Ears should also be monitored daily and kept clean and free from excess wax.

From a practical point of view it is also advisable to trim off excess hair that might cover the pads of the feet; unless the dog can make contact with the ground with its actual pads, it will obviously be difficult for the dog to get a grip. This can be quite harmful to heavy puppies with supple bones.

Nails must be kept short, and here again the puppy must be made accustomed to this manicuring from a very early age. Disaster can result from tackling a twelve-month-old Pekingese for the first time with nail scissors.

Especially for Puppies

In the puppy it is necessary only to keep the coat free from minor tangles that all too quickly become huge mats if not removed. The first essential for successful grooming is having the correct equipment. I recommend using a medium-textured pure bristle brush, a wide-tooth comb, a spray of water-based dressing, talcum powder and cotton, plus a pliable slip lead.

When your puppy is about ten weeks old, in addition to grooming its body coat as I have suggested, you can begin to "train" the hair about the head. This should be done by grooming the hair on the top skull as flat as possible, and the hair behind the ears should be groomed outward and forward to help create the impression of width, with the ear fringes framing the face.

Grooming and Handling—Inseparables

The grooming and handling of the Pekingese varies considerably from other breeds of Toy dogs because the breed holds fast to many traditions that have been created through the years. However, as in most breeds, good grooming and good handling develop from a thorough knowledge of the virtues and faults of a breed. A little sympathy and respect for the breed's true characteristics can also help considerably. Those who have achieved success and established a reputation for being expert in the art of presenting and handling a particular breed have learned why the coat is groomed in a certain fashion or style. Regardless of how natural and effortless the experts appear to present and handle their dogs, it would be foolish to overlook the fact that every stroke of the brush and movement of the hand is calculated and done for a special reason. With the correct equipment, a sound knowledge of the breed, the desire to learn and the ability to practice, there is no reason why good grooming and handling should not be within the capabilities of most.

156

At. St. Aubrey-Elsdon the emphasis has always been on spaciousness in the kennel. Shown here is a range of stalls with wire mesh divisions so that the tenants can see one another. While cages are ideal for sleeping quarters to confine dogs at night, they should be allowed as much freedom as possible during the day.

A range of outdoor runs should always be provided; if possible, a large grass paddock where the Pekingese can romp and play as a group is ideal to develop strength and temperament.

Good grooming and handling should never be confused with incorrect and exaggerated presentation and meaningless and unnecessary gestures. It should be the aim of every handler to expose his dog looking its best and make himself as inconspicuous as possible. Competition should be between exhibits and not handlers. The great handlers of our time present their charges in such a way that the judge's eye is immediately drawn to *their dog* and not themselves. If a handler is more noticeable than his dog, his talent is usually outweighed by his sense of exhibitionism.

During the last few years, with the number of dogs that have developed coats of ridiculous lengths of the wrong texture, there also seems to have developed internationally a tendency to attach more importance to hair than any other feature of the breed.

Good grooming and handling should go together in the daily routine of show dogs. If a dog is taught how to stand and move correctly while being prepared or kept in condition for shows, it will save many frustrating and wasted hours at dog shows. It is important that the time spent on grooming at a dog show should be devoted entirely to making the dog look as attractive as possible. Nail cutting, ear cleaning and removing knots and tangles from the coat should all have been taken care of before leaving home. Grooming should be made as comfortable and enjoyable an experience as possible for both handler and exhibit at a dog show. If the handler is relaxed and confident, his dog well trained and well presented, the dog will react with the same confidence.

The only trimming that should be carried out on the Pekingese, as I have said earlier, is under the pads of the feet. In removing this coat, however, care should be taken to avoid trimming the toe fringes because they are an important Pekingese characteristic. A great deal is said, and in some cases done, about trimming the topskull with razors and scissors. This is wrong and can produce some truly unsightly results. The texture and growth pattern on the skull requires only correct and regular grooming to create a natural flat topskull.

Getting Groomed to Show

Having washed the underparts of the body and the feet, cut the nails, cleaned the ears and removed the surplus coat from under the pads a day prior to the show, your Pekingese should be ready to enjoy its show grooming.

First, place the leash loosely around the dog's neck, allowing it to find a natural and comfortable position. You will need to check this from time to time during grooming. If the lead is put on after the grooming is completed, it does not find its correct position and can destroy all your grooming efforts.

Stand the dog on four legs on a table covered with a towel. It is important for the surface to be firm and not of too smooth a nature, which can cause the dog to slip.

Wash the face and wrinkle with a solution made from one teaspoon of salt and one pint of water. Make sure that the wrinkle and stop are perfectly clean and dry with cotton. The face should be the first, and also the last, part of the

A well laid out kennel with ample room and light and excellent facilities for daily grooming.

grooming. As a final touch, the wrinkle should be combed forward (away from the eyes) with a fine-tooth comb.

Spray the topskull, ears (particularly behind the ears), the rest of the body, tail and trousers with coat dressing—just damping it, though, not wetting it right through—and continue to do so during the grooming. You will learn very quickly that your best results will come when you spray lightly. Brush the coat on the skull back flat, toward the neck, making sure that your brushing starts at the skull and not the forehead. This very common mistake can have the exact opposite effect to the one desired, making the coat stand up rather than lie flat on the skull.

Make sure the ear fringes are free of tangles, and start brushing from the back of the ear in a slightly upward and forward direction. The ears should frame the face, and the fringes should never be brushed higher than the level of the topskull.

Spray the chest and brush downward, making sure that the hair between the shoulders is free from tangles. Repeat the process, starting from between the legs, and hold the coat with the left hand, gradually releasing the coat as you brush and work upward toward the chin.

The body from the skull to the base of the tail should be brushed with the growth of the coat (that is, from skull to tail). This enables the tail to rest on the back and not give the impression that the dog is higher at the back than in the front. The topline should be level to support the tail as it flows over the back. Brush the coat on the sides of the body slightly upward and forward, creating a broad chest. The coat from the end of the ribs and over the loin and the hind legs should be brushed with the natural growth of the coat and never against it. The Pekingese should appear to be heavy in front and light behind. The grooming should follow a pear-shape pattern so that, after a correct grooming, when the dog shakes itself, the coat should fall into a natural shape and style.

The coat on the back of the hind legs (which we call "trousers" or "breeches") should be raised, and the same method of grooming applied as to the chest, starting from the body outward and down.

Continue to spray the coat gently as you groom. Place the tail over the back and brush toward the head. A little talcum powder can be sprinkled behind the ears, on the tail and trousers, and then brushed out.

If your grooming style is correct, you should have been able to create a picture with your brush just as an artist does with a paintbrush. A coat regularly groomed in the correct direction will grow into the style you have created, but it must be done regularly.

While grooming, adjust the lead to its most comfortable position on the dog, which should be under its neck. The lead should hang loosely from under the chin and not from the back of the head because this will create the opposite effect to what you have been working to achieve with the topskull.

Before your dog is ready to go into the ring, give it an opportunity to drink some water and make sure the eyes and face are clean and dry.

An excellent suggestion is to have a photograph of one of the famous dogs in full bloom near your grooming table at home. It should also be borne in mind that the superb examples of presentation seen in photographs have not been achieved in a single grooming session. They are the result of patience and regular, correct grooming methods.

Handling and Showmanship

Hands play a very important part when handling any animal. The touch should be firm but gentle. Since Pekingese are judged on the table by tradition, it is important for your dog to be taught to stand correctly and for you, as a handler, to know when it is not standing correctly. There is no more beautiful sight than seeing a well-groomed Pekingese standing firmly on four legs and allowing the judge to examine it without any interference from the handler. We often see ridiculous examples of the handler trying to show the judge the length of back or the strength of the dog's front or rear legs. This is not good handling. It quite often distorts the dog and irritates the judge.

Brushes, combs, toys and tidbits have their place but should never become a hindrance to the handler or a nuisance to fellow competitors. In the last few years exhibitors have developed a tendency to kneel down in the ring, propping their Pekingese up and constantly brushing their ears and tails. In days past in England, ladies of the breed such as the Allens, Ashton-Crosses and de Pledges would never have been seen on their knees! Their dogs stood naturally on the floor, proud and unaided, occasionally glancing up at their handlers for direction. In those days the picture was completely dignified and a joy to watch, proving, perhaps, that we still have a lot to learn about presenting and handling the Pekingese. If we remember to "reveal the art and conceal the artist," we could come up with a better picture—and with a lot less effort.

For centuries Pekingese have been enjoying gracious living and, hardy though they are, Pekingese are quite unashamed about their affection for luxury. This charming study shows Can. Ch. Genderlee Shoot relaxing at home, one of several well-known winners to have been housed in the Mingchen Canadian Kennel of Olivia Derbyshire and Louise Pearce. Shoot was a son of Eng. Ch. Cherangani Bomber and was bred by Geoffrey Davies.

9

Special Care
and Training
for the Pekingese

$\mathbf{T}$HE PEKINGESE may be classified as a Toy breed, but please do not think that your Pekingese is a delicate soul that must be pampered and cosseted. Of course it will enjoy your pandering to its every whim, but it is a tough little character with a hardy constitution and will be equally at home lounging in a luxury apartment as it would galloping over the rolling hills of a country home.

The Pekingese is totally adaptable and will fit in with almost any life-style, yet you will never really feel that you own your Pekingese as you would most other breeds. It will let you know that it is allowing you to live with it! There is a big difference.

When it comes to special care, you need only groom your Pekingese regularly, as detailed earlier, paying special attention to eyes, ears and coat in general.

From an early age the Pekingese should be taught to walk to heel on a leash. This will make it a pleasure to live with, whether it be Best in Show winner or devoted companion.

Other than this, no special training is necessary. Centuries of civilization have buried the more common canine instincts very deeply in the Pekingese psyche. The Pekingese will not be tempted to chase cattle or sheep, or go off wandering in search of worldly pleasures. It will be quite happy with its domestic situation, provided the situation is up to its expectations. In many ways the Pekingese is quite the easiest breed with which a human can live.

CARTOON   By J. C. WALKER
MY KINGDOM FOR A PEKE!

When the news broke that Mary de Pledge had refused 10,000 guineas (approximately $20,000) offered by Nigel Aubrey-Jones for her famous Ch. Caversham Ku Ku of Yam, the press had a field day. All the prominent daily papers of the day carried the story of this priceless little dog, reporters hounded Miss de Pledge and Ku Ku was photographed with actresses and film stars.

Today the offer would be considered a substantial one, yet the year in question was 1956! The above cartoon appeared in the South Wales *Echo,* whose cartoonist was obviously unimpressed by such a valuable dog.

10

The Character
of the Pekingese

THE PEKINGESE is a breed of unlimited intelligence and like no other. While it is perfectly happy to go along with most of the demands made on it by its master or mistress, should a suggestion not be to its liking, it will not think twice about digging in its heels and "turning a deaf ear." Its imperial inheritance has left it with a convenient stubborn streak, and it will never be afraid to display it.

This slight aura of unpredictability is part of the Pekingese's charm, and if you are seeking a breed that does what it's told immediately every time and without question, then a Pekingese is not for you.

The breed can be a little trying at times when it comes to feeding. Pekingese are not gluttons. They are delicate eaters befitting their noble ancestry, and they may have fads and fancies with their meals. My advice is to establish a feeding regime that suits you and stick to it until such time as your Pekingese disapproves. It is then up to you to find out what exactly will be acceptable to the palate of His Lordship.

Pekingese kept in groups are not, on the whole, a quarrelsome breed, and many households keep large numbers—males and females—together without incident. Naturally, as with all breeds, when several are kept as a pack, a natural "pecking order" has to be established, and the dogs will sort this out for themselves quite naturally. You will soon be able to work out for yourself which is number one by the deference and respect shown it by the others.

The Pekingese has, fortunately, retained many of the characteristics that were bred into it in the Imperial Palace, none more so than the ability to entertain and amuse.

Ch. Chik T'Sun of Caversham

Ch. Ku Chi of Caversham
Ch. Caversham Ku Ku of Yam
Regina of Yam
Ku Chik of Caversham
Ch. Caversham Ko Ko of Shanruss
Ko-Lee of Caversham
Mo-Lee of Caversham
CH. CHIK T'SUN OF CAVERSHAM
Puff Ball of Chungking
Ch. Ku Chi of Caversham
Marigold of Elfann
Naxos Ku Chi Fille of Caversham
Wingco of Sherringham
Psyche of Naxos
Rena of Ifield

166

11

The Westminster Best in Show Pekingese

Mention WESTMINSTER and you incite an aura of mystique to which all dog enthusiasts can relate. The annual Westminster Kennel Club dog show, held every February in New York City's Madison Square Garden, is both show business and high drama translated to the dog show idiom. This great show has been held annually without interruption since 1877 and is second only to the Kentucky Derby, and that by just two years, as the oldest continuously held sporting event in the United States. Indeed, the first Westminster show predates the establishment of the American Kennel Club by seven years!

Dog fanciers shoulder all sorts of hardships to be able to come to Westminster. Even after arriving in New York, exhibitors are frequently beset by trial and inconvenience. But regardless of weather, traffic, high prices and all the rest of it, dog people come to their own special mecca because, well—because it's Westminster.

Winning at the Garden is a dream shared by the entire dog fancy. Whether in the classes, for Best of Breed competition or beyond, almost everyone nurtures a Westminster fantasy. Very few have actually lived the dream, but in the long history of the most exalted dog show of them all, three unforgettable Pekingese have reigned supreme over the most glittering assembly of quality the dog sport can muster.

Ch. St. Aubrey Dragonora of Elsdon

Am. & Eng. Ch. Etive Copplestone Pu Zin Julier
Ch. Laparata Celestial Star
Laparata Celeste
Am. & Can. Ch. St. Aubrey Laparata Dragon
Laparata Francois
Laparata Miranda
Laparata Celeste
CH. ST. AUBREY DRAGONORA OF ELSDON
Ch. Who's Who of Wanstrow
Knostro Tyger Tyger
Fanchon of Knostro
Can. Ch. St. Aubrey Knostro Sandrine
Thimble of Yewstone
Knostro Charm's Pippa
Rio's Charm of Knostro

Pekingese have often prevailed in the Toy Group and at least fourteen such prizes have been conferred on the breed since 1930.

This honor roll of Pekingese Toy Group winners at Westminster includes such memorable animals as Mrs. James Austin's Tang Hao of Caversham Catawba, John Royce's Kai Lo of Dah Lyn, Dorothy Quigley's Ch. Jai Son Fu of Orchard Hill, John Brown's Ch. Dan Lee Dragonseed, Constance Sherman's Ch. Beaupres Tomsjoy Lea Chim and Mrs. Walter Jeffords's and Michael Wolf's Ch. Yang Kee Bernard, among others.

Elsewhere in this book is related the memorable contest between the Pekingese Ch. Phantom of Ashcroft and the White Bull Terrier Ch. Haymarket Faultless competing for that coveted plum. That two of the most prominent judges of the day were hopelessly deadlocked and a referee needed to be called in to render the final decision is a matter of dog show history. The Pekingese bowed on this day, and it would take forty-two years before the barrier would be broken.

Curiously, no Toy dog took a Garden Best before 1956 when the Toy Poodle Bertha Smith's Ch. Wilber White Swan, won the important first under judge Paul Palmer, guided by Anne Hone Rogers (now Mrs. James Edward Clark). Just a year later the Toy Group representative at Westminster was a dog whose name would live in the history of the dog sport forever: the great Ch. Chik T'Sun of Caversham, bred by Mary de Pledge and Herminie Lunham and imported by Nigel Aubrey-Jones and R. William Taylor. He was owned by Mr. and Mrs. Charles C. Venable and handled by the charismatic Clara Alford. This tiny dog and his diminutive handler would have three chances at the top prize with Group firsts in 1957, 1959 and 1960. It was on his third try that Chik T'Sun turned the trick under judge George Hartman. Westminster was one of some 125 all-breed Bests for this dog, and Chik T'Sun is remembered as one of a handful of animals with over one hundred Bests. Those who saw him could never forget him. His very presence proclaimed Pekingese and show dog at the same time. Truly this grand dog had a formidable impact on the show ring status of the Empress Dowager's favorite.

Twenty-two years would pass before another Pekingese would enter the Westminster Best in Show winners' circle. This time it was a bitch: Ch. St. Aubrey Dragonora of Elsdon, cover model for this book, was owned by a Canadian sportswoman, the late Anne Snelling, and bred by R. William Taylor. Handled to this and many other top wins by William Trainor, Dragonora prevailed under Mrs. Robert V. Lindsay. Interestingly, this was Mrs. Snelling's second Westminster Best. Her memorable Irish Water Spaniel Ch. Oaktree's Irishtocrat won in 1979 under judge Henry Stoecker. Dragonora's triumph was, however, the first and to today she remains the only bitch of *any Toy breed* that went to the top at Westminster in the long history of this venerable event.

And now we come to 1990 and the one hundred and fourteenth edition of this supreme spectacle of the dog sport. As with the other 113 Westminsters before it, the cream of dogdom gathered to vie for the prize everyone wants. When all the contestants had left the field, the third Pekingese to win Westmin-

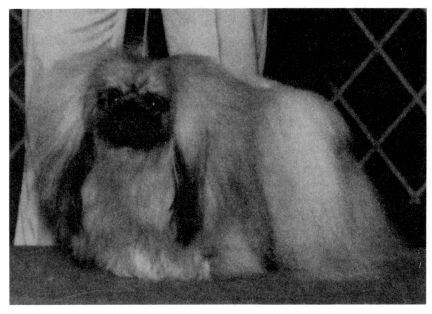

Ch. Wendessa Crown Prince

Can. Ch. St. Aubrey Dragonfly of Elsdon
Am. Can. Ch. St. Aubrey Sunburst of Elsdon
St. Aubrey Sun Queen of Elsdon
Am. Ch. Briarcourts Rule Britannia
Aust. Ch. Gilgai Stormy Boi
Cansue Kaylee
Camsue Amand
CH. WENDESSA CROWN PRINCE
Ch. Laparata Celestial Star
Am. & Can. Ch. St. Aubrey Laparata Dragon
Laparata Miranda
Ch. Wendessa Princess Lyzette
Am. Ch. Colhamdorn C'est Si Bon of Toydom
Am. Ch. Lady Farrah of Fourwinds
Dragon Lady of Fourwinds

ster remained to savor its victory: Ch. Wendessa Crown Prince, owned by Edward B. Jenner and bred by Wendy Bramson. The dog was handled to this coveted award by Luc Boileau over a field that included some of the strongest show dogs of the day.

The judge for the 1990 event was Frank Sabella, one of the sport's most admired authorities. Mr. Sabella is a former professional handler of peerless reputation and an internationally acknowledged connoisseur of the Toy breeds.

As with Mrs. Snelling, owner of Dragonora, Mr. Jenner celebrated his second Westminster Best with the triumph of Crown Prince. In 1973 the legendary Standard Poodle Ch. Acadia's Command Performance, which he co-owned with Jo An Sering, was Best under Mrs. Augustus V. Riggs IV. On this day the Poodle was guided by the 1990 judge Frank Sabella.

Chik T'Sun, Dragonora and Crown Prince represent the cream of the Pekingese breed and are eloquent testimony to the global character of the fancy. Chik T'Sun, imported from England; Dragonora, a product of Canada; and Crown Prince, an American-bred, demonstrate the close cooperation between the fancies of three great dog-showing countries. Their quality and the record of their achievements show the heights that can be reached by dogs of unquestioned excellence.

As you can see, Pekingese account for a considerable part of the history, color and panache of the Westminster show. From the earliest days to the present, this enigmatic aristocrat of dogdom has made its presence felt at America's premier dog show just as it has in the palaces of the Forbidden City and in the homes and hearts of dog lovers around the world.

"Mirror, mirror on the wall . . . I'm the fairest of them all!"

A Century
of Pekingese History

Tracing the Tail Male Line from Ah Cum to Ch. Wendessa Crown Prince

AH CUM	YU TUO OF PEDMORE
GOODWOOD PUT SING	YUSEN YU CHUO
CH. GOODWOOD CHUN	PUFF BALL OF CHUNGKING
MANCHU TAO TAI	CH. KU CHI OF CAVERSHAM
CH. CHU ERH OF ALDERBOURNE	CH. CAVERSHAM KU KU OF YAM
CH. CHUTY OF ALDERBOURNE	CH. COPPLESTONE KU ZEE OF LOOFOO
CH. CHOO TAI OF EGHAM	CH. COPPLESTONE PU ZEE
TAN CHOO OF EGHAM	CH. COPPLESTONE PU ZIN
TAN QUI OF ALDERBOURNE	CH. ETIVE COPPLESTONE PU ZIN JULIER
CH. TAI CHOO OF ALDERBOURNE	CH. LAPARATA CELESTIAL STAR
CH. TAI YANG OF NEWNHAM	CH. ST. AUBREY LAPARATA DRAGON
CH. YU CHUAN OF ALDERBOURNE	CH. ST. AUBREY DRAGONFLY OF ELSDON
TAI CHUAN OF ALDERBOURNE	CH. ST. AUBREY SUNBURST OF ELSDON
YU TUO OF ALDERBOURNE	CH. BRIARCOURT'S RULE BRITANNIA
	CH. WENDESSA CROWN PRINCE

Ch. Ralshams Aristocrat went to New Zealand, where he became a champion for Hazel Rigden. He was sired by Ch. Etive Master Chimes and out of a daughter of Ch. Laparata Celestial Star and the full sister to Ch. Ralshams Lovely Lady.

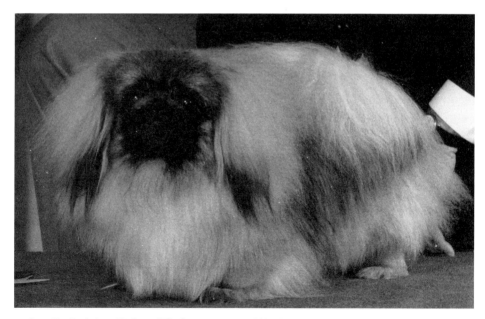

Am. Ch. St. Aubrey Toyboy of Elsdon was a son of Mayfly out of the British import Micklee Rozmiriz of St. Aubrey. He was owned by Edward B. Jenner.

Bibliography of Books on the Pekingese

Ayscough, Florence, *The Autobiography of a Chinese Dog*. Boston: Houghton Mifflin, 1926. With writing-brush sketches by Lucille Douglass.

Collier, V. W. F. *Dogs of China and Japan in Nature and Art*. London: Heinemann, 1921.

Denlinger, Milo G. *The Complete Pekingese*. Silver Spring, Md.: Denlinger's, 1957.

Dixey, A. C. *The Lion Dog of Peking*. 2nd ed. London: Peter Davies, 1931.

Godden, Rumer. *The Butterfly Lions: The Story of the Pekingese in History, Legend and Art*. New York: Viking, 1978.

Hill, Herminie Warner. *Pekingese*. London: Foyle, 1970.

Howe, Elsa, and Howe, Ellic. *The Pekingese Scrapbook*. London: Chapman and Hall, 1954.

Hubbard, Clifford L. B. *The Pekingese Handbook*. London: Nicholson and Watson, 1951.

Ironside, Margaret. *Lung Chung*. London: Home and Van Thal, 1946.

Jacob, Naomi. *Prince China*. London: Hutchinson, 1955.

Jeans, Angela. *Harry the Peke*. London: Black, 1936.

Johns, Rowland, ed. *Our Friend the Pekingese*. New York: Dutton, 1933.

Johnson, Burges. *Sonnets from the Pekingese*. New York: Macmillan, 1935.

Katz, Rose Marie. *This Is the Pekingese*. Jersey City, N.J.: T. F. H. Publications, 1962.

Miller, Madeline. *Pekingese As Pets.* Jersey City, N.J.: T. F. H. Publications, 1956.

Munnings, Alfred. *The Diary of a Freeman.* London: Cassell, 1953.

Nicholas, Anna Katherine. *The Pekingese.* Chicago: Judy, 1952.

Quigley, Dorothy A. *The Quigley Book of the Pekingese.* New York: Howell, 1964.

Scott, Alice. *How to Raise and Train a Pekingese.* New York: Sterling, 1959.

Soutar, Andrew. *A Chinaman in Sussex.* London: Hutchinson, 1931.

Vlasto, John A. *The New Popular Pekingese.* London: Popular Dogs, 1932.

Vlasto, John A. *The Popular Pekingese.* London: Popular Dogs, 1949. Chapter on "Pekes in America" by John B. Royce.

Vlasto, John A. *The Popular Pekingese.* London: Popular Dogs, 1958. Revised by Mary de Pledge.

Vlasto, John A. *The Popular Pekingese.* New York: Arco, 1962.

Whitlock, Brand. *Little Lion.* New York: Appleton-Century, 1937.